kitchen harvest

kitchen harvest

A COOK'S GUIDE TO GROWING ORGANIC VEGETABLES, FRUITS, AND HERBS

SUSAN BERRY

photographs by
STEVEN WOOSTER

illustrations by
MADELEINE DAVID

LAUREL
GLEN

San Diego, California

In memory of my grandmother, Alice Lee Jones, a good gardener and a great cook, and her two daughters: my mother, Patti, and my aunt, Mary.

Laurel Glen Publishing
An imprint of the Advantage Publishers Group
5880 Oberlin Drive, San Diego, CA 92121-4794
www.advantagebooksonline.com

All notations of errors or omissions should be addressed to Laurel Glen Publshing, editorial department, at the above address. All other correspondence (author inquiries, permissions and rights) concerning the content of this book should be sent to Frances Lincoln Ltd., 4 Torriano Mews, Torriano Avenue, London NW5 2RZ.

ISBN 1-57145-760-7

Library of Congress Cataloging-in-Publication Data available upon request

Printed in Singapore

1 2 3 4 5 06 05 04 03 02

contents

PLANNING THE GARDEN

Just a few of the many edible plants you can grow on a small patio. The selection here includes two types of beans, chard, cabbages, zucchini, arugula, and beets, as well as raspberries and blueberries.

There is a surprisingly wide range of edible plants that you can grow successfully in containers, but almost all need a sunny position. If you are growing edible plants in containers for the first time, it is best to concentrate your energies on those that are relatively easy to grow. Herbs are ideal, as they will grow well in even the smallest containers, and a windowsill will suffice for a good range of different culinary herbs, such as parsley, chives, sage, thyme, and basil. Among the easier vegetables are most salad greens, radishes, potatoes, zucchini, tomatoes, and French and pole beans. Of the fruits, strawberries usually do well in containers. Most tree fruits are more demanding, but it is still enjoyable to try one or two in pots.

Not all edible plants are hardy, and those that are tender need more care if you are growing them in a cold climate. You will need to sow the seeds indoors early so that the plants get the longest possible time for ripening. If you are growing tender fruit trees, for example, you may need to overwinter them indoors in very cold weather or wrap the containers in bubble wrap to provide protection against light frosts.

If you are interested in growing produce in containers, you probably do not have a great deal of space. When deciding what to grow, you need to determine how many containers you can position in a reasonably sunny place and then plan what you plant accordingly. There is no point in raising vast quantities of seedlings if there is no space to plant them!

SMART SPACE

Grow climbing varieties if you can, as they take up vertical rather than horizontal space. However, because a grapevine will cast shade under the foliage, other vegetables will not be able to grow underneath its

OPPOSITE Look for unusual varieties, such as 'Lockies Perfection' (top), a cucumber, and 'Long Red Florence' (bottom), a scallion, as experimenting is half the fun of growing edible plants in containers.

canopy. Site this away from your growing space. Tomatoes are clearly among the best container-grown crops, as indeed are outdoor cucumbers. You can even grow tomatoes in hanging baskets if you wish. You can also use hanging baskets for lettuce, strawberries, herbs, and even arugula and radishes. Remember that they dry out very quickly, so plentiful watering will be necessary in hot weather. Moisture retainer, mixed with the growing medium, will help to combat water loss.

It is important to make the best use of a small space, so ideally you need to plan successive sowings, reusing containers as you harvest the crops. You can interplant larger, later maturing crops with smaller, faster growing ones. For example, radishes are very fast growing and can be planted in and among slower growing plants, such as beans. You can plant some vegetables and fruits among flowering plants: for example, strawberries with lettuce and pansies. If you lose a few edible plants in a container to pests or diseases, fill the container up with a smaller crop or with flowers, rather than leaving the container half empty. Make or buy staging so that you can create a tier of containers.

WHAT TO GROW

You can grow almost any vegetable or fruit in a container, but consider what is sensible or worthwhile to grow. The choice of vegetables, fruits, and herbs in this book has been determined by what tastes so good that a small quantity is sufficient. There is little point in growing staple crops that are relatively inexpensive to buy. Look for interesting varieties, such as striped tomatoes, yellow carrots, or unusually shaped chilies (see individual entries for specific suggestions), since half the fun of growing edible plants in containers is showing off your crop.

ORGANIC METHODS

In commercial growing, chemicals have, for the most part, replaced organic methods in order to keep pests and diseases from ravaging the crops. Organic gardening demands more personal attention than the chemical approach. However, precisely because you have a tiny garden growing under your nose, you will see problems early on and can deal with them quickly and efficiently. If your container garden is on a balcony, you should not be troubled by slugs and snails (unless a careless bird

drops one by mistake!). However, if you have a ground-level terrace or patio, you will have to watch out for them (see pages 28–9).

You can now buy a good range of organic fertilizers (see page 140) by mail order or via the Internet, or you can use well-rotted manure or homemade compost to feed your plants.

choosing varieties

When you grow edible plants in containers, you enter the farming world in microcosm, and you learn some interesting lessons as a consequence. In recent years there has been an emphasis on breeding vegetables and fruits that are commercially useful, and research has been directed toward maximizing profit for the farmer. As your own producer of limited supplies of food, you are probably more interested in flavor than yield, and your choice of variety should be made with this in mind. In the days before the profit motive became such an issue, this principle applied to many of the smaller commercial growers, as well.

You will find that many of the old varieties give you the intensity of flavor you desire. However, one of the benefits of modern breeding has been to create varieties that are more resistant to pests and diseases. When you have lost your entire crop of one particular plant, you realize that this is a major issue!

By far the most important aspect of choosing varieties for containers is the amount of space that the plants need, so look for dwarf varieties that will give you a good yield. However, the considerations of space should not keep you from experimenting with a range of varieties. Individual vegetable, fruit, and herb entries in this book offer suggestions as to what you might best grow.

SAVING SEEDS   If you grow naturally pollinated varieties rather than F1 hybrids, you can save the seeds of your own plants for next year's crop. With F1 hybrids, which have been purpose bred, the progeny will either not breed true to type or may be completely sterile. If you want to grow open-pollinated varieties, you will probably need to purchase seeds by mail order from

A selection of seeds, demonstrating the many different forms and sizes in which they come. Clockwise, from top left, these are: peas, beans, nasturtiums, kidney beans, garlic, radishes, zucchini, and beets.

a specialty supplier (see page 142). One such potato grower in Scotland maintains 400 varieties of potatoes, for example. While it is interesting to obtain catalogs from foreign seed merchants, bear in mind that they have developed cultivars best suited to the local climate.

If a particular variety you have grown has pleased you and it is not an F1 hybrid, then consider letting a few plants ripen and save their seeds. Since many plants tend to cross-pollinate, if you want to keep the seeds true to type, you need to put a paper bag over the flowerhead and hand-pollinate it yourself by brushing the pollen from one flower onto the reproductive parts of another.

If the seeds are encased in pods, allow these to dry on the plant naturally to ensure the seeds are fully ripe. Then transfer them to paper bags and take them indoors to a warm, dry spot. After that, keep them in a cool, dark place until needed. Some seeds will be unusable after a year, so it is best to use the seeds sooner rather than later.

choosing containers

You can grow edible plants in any container, as long as it is deep enough to allow room for the roots to spread and contains enough growing medium for the uptake of nutrients. What the latter does not contain in the way of nutrients at the outset or loses over the growing period can be supplemented with various types of organic feed.

However, if you are growing edible plants in a small space, a secondary objective is to ensure that you create an aesthetically pleasing display. Since the plants themselves are not grown primarily for their beauty—although some edible plants are ornamental as well as functional—you can make up for this by choosing handsome containers or, at the very least, trying to impose some uniformity and order on the whole display.

For many years organic gardening has involved recycling, and you can do this without turning your balcony or terrace into a junkyard. By all means reuse old cans, but paint them in subtle colors. Old terra-cotta pots have immense appeal, thanks to the attractive faded color they acquire in time and the irregular shapes that they present if hand-thrown. You can turn a brand-new, offensively bright ginger, machine-made, terra-cotta pot into something more subtle by "antiquing" it. Simply paint yogurt onto the pot with a brush and leave it to dry. The bacteria will encourage the formation of algae, and the pot will rapidly acquire a much classier personality!

If you decide to recycle aluminum pots, such as old buckets or wash-tubs, you must make drainage holes in the base first. You can do this with a bradawl and brute force, or you can use a power drill with a metal bit, which is fast but unpleasantly noisy. Drill at least half a dozen large holes for a container with a base 12 in. across and more, proportionally, for a bigger one. Don't forget to scrub out all old pots before using them in order to get rid of any potentially harmful contents. Also, recycled pots from the previous season's plants must all be scrubbed out to keep viruses and other diseases from being passed on.

If you vary the sizes and shapes of the containers, you will be able to group any display more effectively and make better use of the available space. If you have a very tall container, such as an old chimney pot—ideal for deep-rooting vegetables like potatoes or leeks that need earthing up—you can use it for smaller plants. Simply fill most of it with rubble and then top up the last 10 in. or so of the container with compost, the depth depending on what you want to grow.

To maximize the use of space, you can grow edible plants in hanging baskets. Strawberries are a particularly good choice, as are lettuce, arugula, radishes, and many different herbs, particularly the bushy, low-growing ones such as thyme, marjoram, and parsley. Nasturtiums, of which both the flowers and seeds are edible, also do very well in hanging baskets, although they are susceptible to blackflies.

OPPOSITE Even a relatively small container, such as an old bucket, will be large enough to produce a good crop of pole or French beans.

BELOW LEFT Recycled metal pots— a washtub, bucket, watering can, coal scuttle, and colander—are all suitable containers.

BELOW RIGHT A collection of various sizes and shapes of terra-cotta pots, including a window box and a special strawberry planter.

It is important when growing edible plants to ensure that the container holds enough growing medium for the plant to develop successfully. To this end, the depth of the container is as important as the diameter, particularly for root crops, plants that need earthing up, and fruit trees. Small, fast-growing plants can be grown in relatively small containers (mustard and watercress, some salad crops, radishes, and herbs can be grown in 8-in.-diameter pots), but generally the minimum size is 10 in. in diameter with a similar depth. Root vegetables do best in much deeper containers (around 18 in. deep, at minimum) to ensure the roots have room to grow to their full length.

planting medium

The medium in which you grow your edible plants will determine how well they grow, so it is important to do your research carefully if you want to have something to pick at the end of all the hard work of sowing, watering, and feeding. The general kind of multipurpose compost provided by plant nurseries is not organic, so if you want to ensure your plants are fully organic, buy your compost from a specialty supplier, look for compost that has been approved by an appropriate organization, or make up your own planting medium (see page 140). There are a number of organic products that form the bulky base, including coir (coconut fiber) and wood products, to which grit, potash, and lime are added in varying quantities, according to the formulation needed. The multipurpose formulation is adequate for most vegetables, fruits, and herbs, as most of them grow well in soil that has an average level of acidity. This is soil with a pH rating (by which the level of acidity/alkalinity is graded) of 6–7. A lower pH indicates a higher acidity, a higher pH, higher alkalinity.

PLANT PREFERENCES   Brassicas like a more alkaline soil and need a pH of around 7, so you may need to add a little lime to the compost. You can buy this in bags, and you will need to add only a tablespoonful of lime to the average 12-in.-diameter container. Blueberries like very acid soil and you will have to use an ericaceous (acid) compost for them rather than a standard mix. You can also make your mix more acidic by adding recycled peat. Remember that in hard-water areas, watering with tap water can reduce the level of acidity, and if you are growing plants that prefer acidic conditions, it may be best to collect rainwater in a barrel.

TESTING ACIDITY LEVELS

If you are in doubt as to the pH level of your potting medium, you can test it with an over-the-counter testing kit, in which a small sample of the medium is mixed with liquid in a test tube. This liquid turns color and you can determine the pH levels by comparing the colors with those on the accompanying chart. Corrections to the acidity levels can be made by adding lime or mushroom compost to increase the alkalinity, while leaf mulch or well-rotted organic material will increase the acidity.

**POTTING MEDIUM
LONGEVITY**

Bear in mind that any planting medium loses its nutrients after a short time—they are leached out through watering and rainfall—so it is best to buy or make it in small quantities rather than to keep bags for months, by which time most of the nutrients will have disappeared.

BASIC CULTIVATION

equipment

When you start to produce crops in containers, the first thing you will need is the equipment. This does not amount to much: enough containers of different sizes, a small trowel and fork, a few pencils to act as dibbers, a watering can (and possibly a hose if you have a large patio or terrace), a small sprayer, and seed trays and blocks, as well as a propagator if you want to grow more exotic vegetables. If you are going to make your own compost, you will need a container with a capacity of at least 1 cu. yd. to generate sufficient heat to accelerate the rotting

You will need a small selection of basic equipment and a few tools. Essential items are a watering can and handheld sprayer, trowel and fork, pruning shears, pruning saw, scissors, and a garden knife, as well as garden wire and string.

process. It should also have a lid to keep in the warmth. If you have enough room, it is also a good idea to have a barrel to collect rainwater, as some plants are sensitive to the lime content in tap water in hard-water areas.

To extend your crop and keep off slugs and snails, cloches—even improvised ones made from cut-down, clear, plastic bottles—are useful. When using canes, put a stopper on the end for safety. Do not forget plastic labels and a permanent marker. If you do not label what you sow, you will fall into the embarrassing trap of not being able to remember what was sown when and where. I made the mistake of thinking my young cosmos plants were actually tomato plants until a kind and more knowledgeable friend pointed this out! Many young seedlings—before they develop their true leaves and colors—look deceptively similar.

In addition to the hardware, you will need a plentiful supply of organic potting medium, some multipurpose organic fertilizer, or the various ingredients of fertilizer if you wish to try to mix your own (see page 140).

Some kind of work surface with a cupboard underneath is really useful, if only to save time clearing things away. A couple of large storage boxes can be pushed under a table that you can use for seed sowing or potting up. To grow seedlings well indoors, you need a lighted area positioned away from direct sunlight.

sowing and planting

If you want some of the more unusual varieties mentioned in this book, you will need to obtain the seeds from specialty growers (see *Suppliers* on page 142). Do not buy too much, as seeds do not keep well after a season or two at most, and it is much better to obtain fresh supplies as and when you need them. These days, you get far fewer seeds in a packet than you used to, so it's unlikely you'll have too many. If you can persuade a friend to grow edible plants, you can swap and share seeds. You need very little in the way of equipment to sow seeds, but if you want to grow plants that originate from hotter climates than your own, you may have to invest in a heated propagator, because some seeds will not germinate below certain temperatures. For the bulk of commonly grown vegetables and herbs, you need little more than a few seed trays, small plastic pots, or compartmentalized seed units. Making use of old margarine or yogurt containers is a cheap and effective way to recycle plastic, provided you remember to punch a few drainage holes in the base of each.

The seeds of different plants vary greatly in size and appearance, but it is primarily the size that affects the way the seed is sown. The seed is a small capsule with all the genetic growing information the plant needs. Once it is provided with favorable conditions—bear in mind that what is favorable to one plant may be death to another!—the trigger to sprout into life will be given. These conditions are the optimum degree of warmth, moisture, and light to which the particular organism has been programmed to respond. Your job is to give the seeds these conditions and then to make sure that they continue to apply. It is no good carefully sowing your seeds and then completely forgetting about them. If you put them on a hot windowsill where they bake in the sun, let the compost dry out, or sluice them with so much water that they drown or turn moldy, your initial outlay will have been in vain.

The basic requirements for seed sowing are:

- enough depth of compost for the roots to form—be careful not to use too much.

- fine enough compost for small seeds and seedlings to be able to force their way through it—it may need to be sieved.

- the right amount of warmth, moisture, and light for germination to begin—seed packets give temperatures and timing.

- to make sure that once germination has begun, the same conditions apply until the seedlings are planted in their final positions.

Not much equipment is needed for sowing seeds, apart from a range of suitable seed trays or pots, a sieve, a dibber, labels, and a permanent marker or pencil. If you want to sow seeds of tender plants, you will find a special propagation unit helpful as well.

If you do not have good overhead light (the ideal situation for seedlings), make sure you turn the trays of seedlings every day to keep them from growing toward the light. If there is not enough natural light, the seedlings will become etiolated, or weak and spindly. Find a position that has more light or invest in daylight bulbs.

DEPTH OF SOWING

Very fine seeds are generally sown on the surface of the potting compost and a fine layer of compost is then sieved over it. Otherwise, you can sow at approximately twice the depth of the seed or check the seed packets, as they almost always give appropriate instructions.

SEED SPACING

If you sow carefully, you can keep seeds from going to waste. However, since not all seeds germinate, you should allow for more than you need—by around fifty percent. If you are lucky and all the seeds grow, you will have to thin the seedlings out to a spacing that will allow the plants to develop properly. This spacing is determined by how big you want the eventual plant to grow. The newly fashionable miniature vegetables are basically plants that are packed in together and harvested while they are very young. They are tender but not always full of flavor—flavor often develops with maturity—and are expensive because twice the amount of seeds are used for half the eventual crop. They are useful for the container-gardening home grower, because packets of seeds are not particularly expensive.

TRANSPLANTING

Most seeds are sown in seed trays and transplanted into their containers when they are large enough to handle—when two true leaves have formed. However, there are a few plants, such as radishes, that dislike being transplanted and these will need to be sown in place. To transplant seedlings, use a fine dibber—a pencil is just right—to remove the seedling from the tray, then pick it up gently by the leaves, as the stem bruises easily. Make a hole in the new compost with the dibber and gently drop the seedling into it. Firm the compost carefully around the newly planted seedling.

ACCLIMATIZING

To produce early crops of plants, you need to put the young plants outside as soon as any frosts are over. Get them acclimatized to outdoor conditions by putting them outside during the day and bringing them in at night for about a week. If you put a minicloche—a cut-down bottle is ideal—over a pot, it will help to keep the plant warm and free from pests and diseases while it is acclimatizing. It will also enable you to grow plants earlier, thereby extending the season.

BASIC PLANTING

Various seedlings and young plants at different stages of growth. It pays to sow seeds successively so that you do not harvest all your plants at once.

When planting in large containers, remember to crock the pot (cover the drainage hole with pebbles or broken shards of pot) to make sure that the holes do not block up with compost and prevent free drainage. Always water plants well and keep them well-watered while they are adjusting to their new home. Choose a container size that is suitable for the growth habit of the plant in question. Fruit trees generally need a container that is 3 in. larger than the rootball of the tree.

feeding

Many edible plants are surprisingly accommodating and will produce some kind of crop with very little help from you. If you want the best tasting plants, you will need to feed them the right types of nutrients at the right time in roughly the right quantities. Each vegetable or fruit has specific demands for certain kinds of nutrients at certain times, since specific nutrients are needed at different stages of growth, such as for leaf, flower, or fruit formation. For example, nitrogen produces leafy growth, and potash aids the production of fruit. While you can make up your own fertilizers in appropriate proportions, it is easier and quicker to buy ready-made ones.

Feeding too frequently with overrich, chemical-based fertilizers makes crops grow larger but they become tasteless in the process. The secret is to find a good source of organic fertilizer that does the job effectively without overdoing it. You can use homemade compost as a useful mulch and also as a supplementary feed, since it may not necessarily contain precisely the right nutrients.

MAKING COMPOST

If you have room to do so, making your own compost is both useful and satisfying. You can buy a compost bin with removable slats that will enable you to draw off the compost when it is ready. All you need to do is store your vegetable and fruit peelings, tea leaves, coffee grounds, and eggshells—but no cooked food—along with any plant waste (but not diseased plants or perennial weeds). Try to layer the ingredients with small amounts of shredded paper or straw. When sufficient heat generates in the bin, bacteria will begin rotting down the waste into a mixture rich in nitrogen. A small amount of compost activator applied to the heap as the layers build up will help to keep it all moving. You will need to keep the top covered to keep the heap from becoming waterlogged, although it is a good idea to moisten the heap periodically so that the contents do not dry out. After about six months, you should have usable compost from it.

Plant foods or fertilizers can be applied either in the form of pellets or granules, or watered direct onto the soil or onto the leaves (foliar feeds). The take-up rate of each of these forms of feed varies; the foliar feeds are the fastest, so they are most useful for providing a quick plant pick-me-up. However, the foliar feeds are not part of the best organic practice in which the growing conditions are improved first.

There are a number of good organic plant feeds available. One of the best is a mixture made from any rich organic matter, such as animal manure, enclosed in a muslin bag and steeped in water for about ten days. The nutrients in the organic matter will disperse into the water, providing you with a useful feed that you can use as needed. Dilute it to the color of weak tea before applying it to the plants.

The potting compost used for planting will last the plants for an average of six weeks, but after that you will need to provide supplementary feeding. This becomes even more important for fruiting plants, including tomatoes, eggplants, and peppers, which need more copious feeding once the fruit starts to form. Generally, you will need to feed these plants every three to four weeks. Each plant entry explains approximately how often to feed the plants and with what.

TYPES OF FOOD

TIME TO FEED

watering

If you grow any plants in containers, watering is a major priority. It is especially important to ensure that edible plants receive regular, generous quantities of water. If you are going to grow them on a balcony or roof terrace, try to place them near a sink, if possible, otherwise you may find yourself increasingly reluctant to water your plants.

Not only does regular, plentiful watering help the plants grow to their full size and develop more succulent leaves and fruits, it will also help prevent pests and diseases. Plants subjected to stress—and irregular watering is a major cause of this—are much weaker. Failure to water on a regular basis will lead to stunted growth, and overwatering to compensate does not help—it simply adds to the stress!

Zucchini are easy to grow and prolific, making excellent use of limited container space. They enjoy a deep, rich growing medium. Eat the surplus male flowers as well as the fruit.

To give you some idea of the amount of water needed, a large barrel, fully planted, would lose up to 1½ gallons of water a day in hot weather. When you water, make sure that you do more than simply wet the top surface of the soil. Fill your pots with compost to roughly 1 in. from the rim, then when you water fully grown plants, fill the container with water to the rim. Any surplus will simply drain away.

Seedlings are particularly susceptible to drought and will need regular watering from a watering can with a fine nozzle. Grouping plants together helps cut down on potential moisture loss through transpiration and makes watering easier. Moisture-retaining seaweed meal can also be used to improve the water-holding capacity of the growing medium. A small handful, mixed in with the growing medium, will be sufficient.

WATERING EQUIPMENT AND DEVICES

All you need is a watering can with a fine nozzle attachment. Watering cans are available in many different styles, but the traditional galvanized metal watering cans (now being reproduced in trendy gardening stores) are perfectly serviceable and look a lot more attractive than plastic ones.

If you have a roof terrace, balcony, or patio, you can install a drip watering system that does the job for you by delivering the water directly to the plants via linked tubing with tiny nozzles. However, the nozzles tend to clog up with growing medium, and it is hard to disguise the tubing effectively, so unless you are away from home often, it is probably better to make the effort to hand-water your plants.

To help gauge water quantities, you can buy small moisture-reading sticks. You insert these into the compost, and they change color when the growing medium starts to dry out. However, edible plants rely on generous amounts of water, so this so-called early warning system may deliver a warning that is a bit on the late side.

WHEN TO WATER

Always water in the early morning or evening on sunny days, because the combination of water and sunlight can scorch the leaves, leaving unsightly brown patches and spoiling a crop of leafy vegetables.

supporting and protecting plants

If you are growing climbing or vining plants, you will need to provide an adequate support system for them, which will be determined by the way the plant climbs. Individual entries for vegetables and fruits include suggestions as to the type of support systems to use.

For climbing plants, such as pole beans, and for tomatoes, peppers, and eggplants, which can be heavy when fully laden with a crop, a strong, well-anchored support system is essential. Other plants that do not climb but that have delicate or floppy stems may also benefit from some support. For dwarf varieties of peas and beans, for example, a simple system of short lengths of brushwood, inserted a few inches deep into the container close to the stem of the plant, will be all that is needed. For taller varieties, angled poles, tied together at the top to form a wigwam shape, are ideal. Alternatively, grow the beans up a trellis or on strings attached to a horizontal support roughly 6 ft. off the ground.

BELOW Cucumbers (left) need to be tied to a strong support, such as a cane. Floppy basil leaves (center) can be contained with a few brushwood twigs. Summer fruits, such as red currants (right), will need to be netted to keep birds from taking the crop.

Fast-growing plants requiring support, such as cucumbers and tomatoes, will need strong canes inserted at the time of planting and then a system of horizontal wires at 6-in. intervals onto which the lateral shoots can be trained as the plant grows. A grapevine will need the sturdiest support system (see page 108), to which the new shoots will need to be tied in, because a fully laden vine at harvesttime can become remarkably heavy. A supporting pergola is ideal and offers a shaded area on hot summer days.

In addition to providing growing support, you will need to give your plants some protection in colder weather. Low-growing vegetables and herbs can be protected with purpose-bought or homemade see-through covers, or cloches, of various description. A cut-down, mineral water container, upturned over a pot, acts as an impromptu cloche and will also double up as protection for young seedlings from slug and snail damage. You can also buy small polytunnels, if you have sufficient space, or individual glass bell or barn cloches. Alternatively, you can cover your crops with various see-through covers made from plastic, fleece, or fine-net film. They are ideal not only for preventing damage from frosts but also for protecting young plants from flying insect pests. However, insect pollination will not take place under these films so remove them from all except self-fertile plants before they flower.

If you are growing tender fruit trees, you will need to consider winter protection for them in cold climates. You can either overwinter the plants indoors, if you have room, or you can wrap the containers in burlap or bubble wrap, which will afford the plants some protection.

Fine netting will be needed in summer to cover most fruit crops—otherwise birds will almost certainly consume them before you get the chance. Make sure the netting is fixed securely.

common pests and diseases

You are not alone in enjoying the flavor of organic produce. Pests of all descriptions may descend on them, eager to get their share of the produce. The good news is that container growing (particularly if you are gardening above ground level) cuts out most soil-borne pests, and good plant management, with appropriate feeding and watering, reduces the likelihood of disease. Watching your plants closely permits you to nip incipient attacks in the bud. To minimize diseases, make sure that all the pots you use are thoroughly cleaned before reuse. The following are the most common pests and diseases, although there is a much wider range that can attack your plants. See individual entries for specific problems.

PESTS   **aphids**   These can be a particular nuisance. They suck the sap from young shoots and often transmit virus diseases in the process. Spray with insecticidal soap or, as a last resort, derris. Encouraging beneficial insects, such as ladybugs, will help control them.

beetles and weevils   These tend to nibble plants, particularly radishes. Either cover the plants with fleece or spray with derris.

caterpillars   These attack the brassica family in particular. Use biological controls, net the crops, or pick them off by hand. Underplanting cabbages with French marigolds helps deter cabbage butterflies.

red spider mites   Mainly a greenhouse pest, this pest damages fruiting vegetables, especially in hot weather. Keep plants humid with frequent spraying. Biological controls can be used under glass.

scale insects   These can attack a wide range of plants. Spray with insecticidal soap.

slugs and snails   These attack the young shoots and leaves of a wide range of plants and will also eat tubers. Use nematodes or stand the pots in a moat of water.

whiteflies   They love brassicas. Plant French marigolds nearby or net the plants. Use biological controls in the greenhouse.

DISEASES

mildews This causes pale blotches on young leaves and yellow areas on older ones. Tips of leaves go gray and die back. Don't overcrowd young plants, particularly lettuce. Spray with sulphur at first signs of disease.

mosaic virus Various kinds attack different vegetables—cucumbers, lettuce, and tomatoes in particular. They cause mottling and puckering of leaf surface, and plants become stunted and may die. Tomatoes will become bronzed and blemished. The best defense is to buy virus-tested seeds. Destroy any affected plants immediately, as the virus spreads rapidly.

DISORDERS

magnesium deficiency Common on tomatoes, this causes leaves to yellow and drop. Caused by high potash feeds. Dress with Epsom salts.

calcium deficiency When plants are deficient in calcium, the blossoms rot. Water regularly so that more calcium is taken up.

premature fruit drop Usually caused by irregular feeding and watering. Improve the feeding and watering regime.

fruit withering Affects cucumbers as a result of poor nutrition. Sometimes caused by rotting.

premature flowering (bolting) Affects spinach, arugula, onions, and Asian brassicas. Caused by inadequate watering in hot conditions.

ORGANIC CONTROLS

derris Use for aphids, beetles, caterpillars, and red spider mites.

pyrethrum Use for caterpillars, whiteflies, leafhoppers, and aphids.

insecticidal soap Use for aphids, red spider mites, and whiteflies.

bordeaux mixture Use for blight.

sulphur Use for powdery mildew.

biological control Various forms exist. Check with organic associations and organic garden suppliers.

grease bands Use on fruit trees to deter pests.

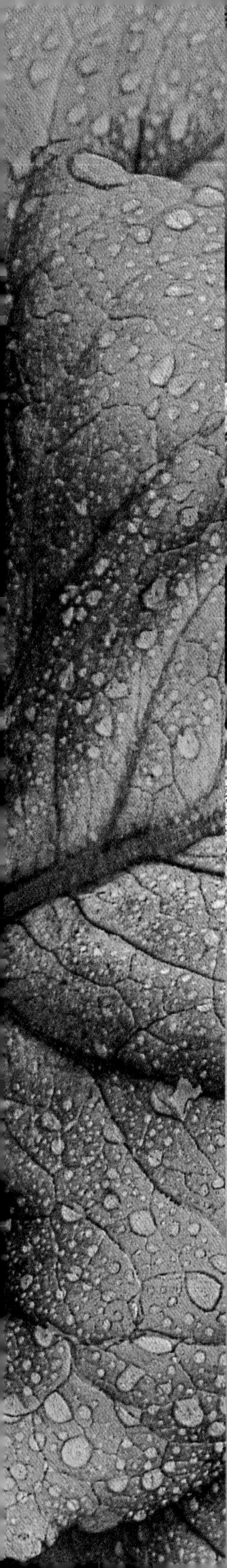

vegetables

roots · stems · leaves ·
fruiting vegetables · salad
crops · other vegetables

potatoes

solanum tuberosum

Potatoes are an excellent source of vitamin C and the B vitamins. They are divided into three groups—earlies, second earlies (or midseason potatoes), and main crops—depending on how long they take to mature. Although potatoes are generally thought of as a large-scale, staple crop, earlies are well worth growing in containers, as they are expensive in stores at this time. Pressure on space tends to preclude growing main-crop potatoes. Early potatoes are easy to grow but need a fairly sunny spot to thrive. Usually, potatoes are planted in the spring, but you can plant them well into summer, and doing so will give you "new" potatoes well into fall.

VARIETIES

There are many unusual varieties of potatoes, as well as the commonly grown ones. Choose double-certified seed potatoes, guaranteed to be both organic and free from viruses and diseases. Earlies take around eighty to one hundred days to mature. Good varieties for containers are: 'Belle de Fontenay': this classic French salad potato, first introduced in 1855, has yellow flesh and a waxy texture; 'Charlotte': another French potato, also good for salads, with waxy flesh; 'Kestrel': a second early introduced in 1992, with good disease resistance; 'Pink Fir Apple': an oddly shaped, pink-skinned potato, with good flavor, but it can be difficult to grow; 'Remarka': a Dutch variety introduced in 1992 with creamy flesh and slightly waxy, with good disease resistance; 'Wilja': another popular Dutch potato, which offers a high yield and is very reliable.

A container of potatoes has been tipped out, showing how the potatoes develop up the stems of the plant. For this reason, earthing up is essential as the plants continue to grow.

CONTAINER SIZE

You can grow potatoes in any deep container. Old buckets, chimney pots, and wine barrels are ideal. Allow a depth of at least 18 in. so that you can earth up (see below) the potatoes as the shoots grow. Plant about five potatoes in an 18-in.-diameter pot.

CULTIVATION

Buy seed potatoes in early spring and keep them in a cool, dry place to sprout, or "chit." This will take a month or so. Once the sprouts are about 1 in. long, you can plant the tubers in containers, with the shoot pointing upward, on a bed of compost about 6 in. deep. Cover them with another 6 in. of compost and continue covering them as the shoots grow—this process is known as "earthing up." The potatoes form from the sides of the growing stem in a pyramid formation.

If light reaches them, the tubers will turn green—thanks to the presence of solanin, a poisonous chemical—hence the need to keep earthing up the stems. Keep the container well watered throughout this period to ensure that the potatoes swell to their full size. Provide an organic feed every couple of weeks.

Soil-planted potatoes are subject to a number of soil-borne diseases, from which container-grown potatoes are free, fortunately. The only possible disease in a container is potato blight, which caused the famine in Ireland in the nineteenth century. It does not seem to occur if you grow earlies.

HARVESTING

Once they flower—roughly three months after planting—the potatoes should be fully formed. You can dig up one plant to check progress or scrabble around to find the first potato without digging up the whole plant. Remember that you can store any potatoes that you do not want to use immediately in a cool, dark place.

POTATOES FOR THE TABLE

Don't peel potatoes. Scrub them and cook them in their skins, where most of the vitamins are concentrated. Different varieties of potatoes are best for particular dishes: waxy potatoes such as 'Charlotte' are excellent for salads and for sautéeing.

sautéed potatoes with garlic and rosemary

This simple dish is delicious and the aroma released while cooking is almost the best part. Simply scrub some new potatoes and boil them in salted water until just tender. Then heat a couple of tablespoonsful of good-quality olive oil in a frying pan, add three chopped cloves of garlic, a couple of sprigs of rosemary, and the seasoning. Add the potatoes, roughly chopped or sliced, and cook over a medium heat until the potatoes start to turn crisp and brown. Serve immediately.

2 cups waxy potatoes

2–3 tbsp. extra-virgin olive oil

3 cloves of garlic

2 sprigs of rosemary

seasoning

warm potato salad

This recipe makes a great light meal, lunch, or appetizer. Boil the potatoes with a little salt until just tender—about twenty minutes. Twelve minutes after putting the potatoes on to boil, put the four eggs on to boil in cold water, and five minutes after that, put the beans on to boil in lightly salted boiling water. In a large bowl, place torn pieces of lettuce as a base. Peel the eggs and cut into quarters, chop the potatoes into rings or quarters, and put the beans in whole. Halve the tomatoes and then add the anchovies, garlic, olives, and seasoning. Dress with a lemon vinaigrette (⅔ cup olive oil, ⅓ cup lemon juice, ¼ tsp. strong mustard, and a pinch of sugar and salt).

2 cups waxy salad potatoes

4 eggs

1 cup snap beans

1 head lettuce

1 cup cherry tomatoes

1 can of anchovies

2 cloves of garlic, crushed

handful of black olives

seasoning

lemon vinaigrette dressing

onion family

*onions (**allium cepa**), leeks (**a. porrum**), garlic (**a. sativum**)*

Although growing large onions is less useful if you are gardening in a confined space, you can successfully grow smaller versions of this valuable family of plants. They include scallions (immature onions), pickling onions, and shallots (*A. cepa*), as well as leeks (*A. porrum*), which you can harvest small, and garlic (*A. sativum*). All members of this family produce swollen leaf bases or bulbs. They are a useful source of vitamin C and phytochemicals, as well as vitamin A, calcium, and iron. Members of the onion family need a sunny spot to ripen well.

VARIETIES

onions   'Stockton Red': red-skinned with mild flavor; 'New York Early': early-maturing and easy to grow.
scallions   'Evergreen Hardy White': popular and can be grown successionally; 'Long Red Florence': long with red skins.
leeks   'Scotland': very hardy.
garlic   'Christo': produces a good yield; 'Russian Red': hardy, with a good flavor.

CONTAINER SIZE

Salad onions, scallions, and chives (a member of the onion family but an herb, see page 126) will all grow well in small pots or troughs, so they are ideal for a window box. Grow onions, leeks, and garlic in a larger container, about 24 in. in diameter and 18 in. deep. Leeks will also do well in a tall, narrow container, such as an old chimney pot, which enables you to earth up the stems as they grow, keeping them long and well blanched.

The onion family does best in slightly alkaline soil and with less nitrogen than most other vegetables. Add a tablespoon of potash to a standard-sized container (12 in. in diameter) of organic compost. To grow onions (*A. cepa*), either sow seeds or plant sets (small bulbs). If you are planting onion sets, plant them in fall with the tips just showing above the growing medium. The benefit of growing smaller onions like scallions is that you can pack them in closely, making good use of container space, and harvest them while they are still immature, before they grow too large. To grow onions from seeds, sow the seeds in early spring in well-

CULTIVATION

ABOVE LEFT Scallions will grow well in small pots, no more than 8 in. in diameter.

ABOVE RIGHT Onions can be raised in individual growing blocks.

firmed growing medium for a summer/fall crop or in late summer for fall/winter use. Onions do not like loose soil, so make sure the growing medium is firmed up well.

To grow leeks (*A. porrum*), sow the seeds in the spring and transplant once the seedlings are about 6 in. tall, making a narrow hole with a dibber into which the seedling can be dropped. Keep earthing the plants up to increase the length of the white shank. Space at 4-in. intervals for smaller leeks.

To grow garlic, plant the cloves in late fall, with the tips just below the surface of the growing medium, spacing the cloves approximately 4 in. apart.

Water all plants of the onion family regularly, and once the bulbs start to swell or the stems are lengthening, feed once a month.

Onion flies can be a nuisance, but covering the plants with fleece will help protect them. Mildew and rotting can also be a problem. Allow plenty of room around the containers to increase air circulation.

HARVESTING   Harvest garlic and scallions in early summer. Harvest onions in fall and leeks from fall onward. You can keep onions and garlic by hanging them in a cool, dry, well-ventilated place.

STORING ONIONS
String onions or garlic together, using a length of raffia or string, knotted to make a loop. Then weave the onion or garlic stems in and out through the loop, adding a new bulb just above the previous one.

spring onion and bacon quiche

This makes a good, light lunch or supper served with green salad and homemade bread.

Grease a small pie pan and line with the pastry. Prick with a fork, weight the base with cooking beans, and bake at 400°F for fifteen minutes. Allow to cool. Grill the bacon until crisp and break into small pieces. Lightly fry the scallions in a little butter. Beat the eggs. Mix the beaten eggs, cream, bacon, and onions together, add the grated cheese and seasoning, and pour into the cooled pan. Lower the oven temperature to 375°F and cook for thirty minutes until the filling has just set—it should be firm to the touch—and is starting to brown.

1 ready-made piecrust

4 slices of bacon

2 tbsp. butter

bunch of scallions (about 8), chopped

2 eggs

⅔ cup sour cream

⅔ cup cheddar, grated

seasoning to taste

vegetable pancakes

Make the pancake batter by putting the flour and seasoning in a bowl and dropping an egg into a well in the middle. Draw the flour in and then add the milk gradually to make a smooth paste. Thin out with milk until it is the consistency of yogurt. Allow the batter to stand for half an hour, and then cook the pancakes in a preheated frying pan greased with melted butter. Turn the pancake onto a plate and place a sheet of waxed paper between each one.

for the vegetable filling

Fry the onion and garlic until golden and soft, and add whatever cold, cooked vegetables you have: snow peas, beans, spinach, kale, and/or finely sliced carrots, for example. Allow to heat for three to four minutes, then add half the cream, half the Parmesan and the herbs, and stir. Cook for another few minutes, and then pour the mixture on top of each pancake, roll, and cover with the remaining Parmesan and a pat of butter. Place in a greased ovenproof dish, pour over the remaining cream, and bake in a preheated 400°F oven for fifteen minutes.

FOR THE PANCAKES

1 cup plain flour

1 large egg

1 cup milk

pat of butter

seasoning to taste

FOR THE FILLING

1 red onion, chopped

2 cloves of garlic, chopped

2 cups cooked vegetables, finely sliced

juice of half a lemon

1 cup cream

4 tbsp. Parmesan cheese

1 tbsp. mixed fresh herbs

seasoning

pat of butter

carrots

daucus carota

A deep window box in a sunny position makes the ideal place to grow carrots. Here 'Amsterdam' carrots have just been pulled.

Hardy biennials, grown as annuals, carrots are full of vitamin A and are a valuable source of other vitamins—B, C, D, E, and K—and potassium. They do well in containers where it is possible to provide the loose, rich soil that they like. There is a wide range of varieties to choose from, some orange, some yellow, some traditionally long, some round. If you harvest them small, they will be ready in ten to twelve weeks.

VARIETIES

There are early-maturing, main-crop, and late-maturing carrots. The first two are most useful for container growing. 'Paris Market' group: small, round carrots, which are quick to mature; 'Amsterdam': slender carrots with smooth skins, also early maturing; 'Chantenay': slightly stumpy carrots for early crops; 'James Scarlet Intermediate': medium-sized main crop; 'Scarlet Nantes': smooth, long-rooted, main-crop carrots.

CONTAINER SIZE

Large, long carrots need a deep container, such as an old chimney pot, to allow room for the roots to develop to their full size. Smaller early carrots can be grown in shallower containers, but ideally they should be at least 9 in. deep.

CULTIVATION

You can extend the season for fresh carrots by sowing in early spring and placing a cloche over the container or by sowing in late summer and using a cloche in early fall. Be aware that carrots are slow

germinators in lower temperatures and need a temperature of at least 45°F to get going. Seeds can be sown without protection from midspring to early summer. Sow the seeds ½ in. deep and thin to 3 in. apart—the thinnings are good in salads. Not all the carrots will grow to the same size, and you will find you have some fully grown ones and some less well-formed ones. The foliage is pretty, so you can sow the seeds with annual flowers and grow the carrots in a mixed ornamental and vegetable container if you wish.

Water carrots regularly to keep the roots from splitting, but be careful not to overwater, as this can cause too much leaf growth at the expense of root formation.

Carrot flies are a serious problem with major crops of carrots because the flies are attracted by the smell of the foliage. Container-grown carrots do not seem to suffer as badly, but growing the carrots under fleece will prevent the problem.

HARVESTING

Harvest the carrots as they reach an appropriate size. Water the container before harvesting those carrots that have grown to maturity so that you do not disturb the remaining ones.

CARROTS FOR THE TABLE

Carrot salads, of one sort or another, make use of the sweetness and crunchiness of young carrots. A good combination consists of carrots, watercress, and mustard leaves. You will need twice the quantity of carrots and watercress to the mustard. Wash and dry the watercress, remove any coarse stalks, and break the rest into smaller pieces. Grate the carrot, snip off the mustard, and mix all the ingredients together. Dress the salad with a good lemon vinaigrette (see page 35). If you make a larger quantity of vinaigrette than you need, keep what is left in an airtight jar in the refrigerator. It will keep for a few days.

beets

beta vulgaris

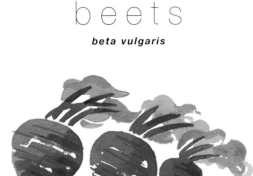

Beets are a rich source of vitamin C, folic acid, and potassium. They do best in cooler weather because the plants are inclined to bolt, or set flowers, in hotter conditions. Some varieties have been developed with bolt resistance however, and these can be grown later in the year. Sow them in succession for a ready supply for summer salads. The beets will be ready roughly ten weeks after sowing if you harvest them small, 2 in. in diameter.

VARIETIES

Beets can be round or long, and red-, white-, or yellow-fleshed.
round 'Boltardy': bolt-resistant, early beets with deep red flesh; 'Golden': orange skin with yellow flesh (you can use the leaves as greens); 'Albina Veredura' (also sold as 'Snowhite'): white flesh.
long 'Cylindra': oval-shaped beets with deep red flesh; 'Cheltenham Green Top': a long, tapering shape, so it is best to grow it in a deep container.

CULTIVATION

Beet seeds are in fact composed of a cluster of seeds. However, you can buy pelleted seeds that will create single plants and are therefore more economical, as they require less thinning. Make several sowings of beets for continuous supplies, sowing 3 in. apart. The seeds are quite large and therefore easy to handle, but you can plant them more closely and then thin out unwanted seedlings. If you sow some seeds in early

spring and cover them with a cloche—a large, clear-plastic bottle cut down makes a good homemade version—you can harvest them small in early summer. Make the other sowings in late spring or early summer for early- and late-summer harvesting. Apply organic fertilizer once a month and keep the compost moist at all times. Birds may take the young seedlings, so protect them with netting.

There are a number of good varieties of beets that will grow well incontainers. For example, 'Pronto,' which can be harvested from midsummer onward.

Pull the beets at different stages of development for a variety of sizes. To harvest them, fork them up carefully and twist off the tops. Do not cut them or they will bleed. You can use the young leaves in salads.

HARVESTING

Beets are normally cooked in their skins, so simply scrub them first and then boil them in lightly salted water until they are tender—usually about thirty minutes for small beets, longer for larger ones. Beets go very well with sour cream and chives. Make a simple salad with these ingredients or make a hot dish by slicing the beets in rings and layering them in a small, buttered, ovenproof dish. Pour enough sour cream over the beets to cover, and bake in the oven at 350°F for fifteen minutes. Sprinkle with chopped chives and parsley or cilantro. Serve warm but not piping hot.

BEETS FOR THE TABLE

If you grow different-colored beets, you can make a colorful salad using sliced beets on a bed of young spinach, arugula, and radish leaves, for example, or any other mix of young green leaves. Dress with a light lemon vinaigrette (see page 35).

chard

***beta vulgaris* cicla group**

Chard, a member of the spinach family, will grow well in containers and provides a valuable source of vitamin C and iron. Ruby chard, with its blood-red leafstalks and midribs, is the most attractive, so is a good choice in limited space. Swiss chard has thick, white midribs and leaf stalks. All spinaches have similarly fleshy green leaves, and they all make deep roots, so give them a deep container for best results. Unlike many vegetables, chard and spinach will do well in light shade, so can be useful in limited space. Winter spinach (*Spinacea oleracea*) is particularly good, as it will crop when there is not much else around.

VARIETIES

There are a few different kinds of ruby and Swiss chard, but spinaches are rarely listed. 'Rhubarb Chard': the best known, with brilliant red midribs and leaf veins, is ornamental as well as edible; 'Rainbow Bright Lights': orange, red, and yellow midribs and leaf veins; 'Fordhook Giant': prolific, larger than usual, robust Swiss chard.

CONTAINER SIZE

A container at least 12 in. in diameter and 12 in. deep is the best size for these vegetables. You can plant two to three in a pot 12 in. across.

CULTIVATION

Sow seeds of chard and summer spinach ½ in. deep in midspring, two or three to a 12-in. pot, and when the seedlings are large enough to handle, thin them out to around 9 in. apart. Avoid overcrowding, as it encourages mildew—as I found when I tried to maximize the space in my containers! Sow spinach seeds in the same way. Summer spinach can be sown from midspring to late spring; winter spinach is sown from late summer for a winter crop. Spinach needs plenty of nitrogen, so top-dress with an organic fertilizer during growth. You can grow spinach as a cut-and-come-again seedling crop (leaving about 3 in. between plants), using the young leaves in salads. Keep well watered at all times and feed with liquid fertilizer once a month. Do not grow close to other plants from the zucchini/cucumber family, as they are all susceptible to the same viruses.

Pull individual leaves when necessary. Use the smallest leaves for salads with other salad greens (see pages 62–9).

BELOW There are several varieties of chard, but generally those with the most colorful midribs are the best for containers. The color in the young rainbow chard (below left) is not fully developed; in a mature plant (below right), the midribs are a rich orange-red.

HARVESTING

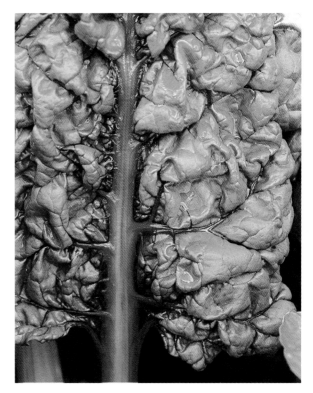

cabbage, kale

brassica oleracea capitata group

These are among the most nutritious vegetables you can grow, but are not universally appreciated. However, even if you don't eat them, they make interesting-looking plants. You can grow them in early spring for fall harvests and in summer for winter harvests. Spring cabbages have looser leaves and are sown in summer for an early-spring harvest. As your space is probably taken up in spring and summer with other crops, winter cabbages could be a good choice. Kales are the hardiest members of the brassica family, and their flavor improves after frost.

VARIETIES

fall cabbages 'Cuor di Bue'; 'Red Drumhead.'
winter cabbages 'January King'; 'Premium Late Flat Dutch.'
dwarf kale 'Green Curled'; 'Redbor'; 'Russian Red.'

CONTAINER SIZE

Plant one cabbage or kale plant in each 8-in.-diameter container, or three in a large window box or grow bag.

CULTIVATION

Sow seeds in late spring to early summer, three to a pot, and thin out to the best seedling in each. Use cloches, fleece, and netting to protect young cabbage seedlings from birds, flying insects, and slugs and snails. Cabbages require more nitrogen than kale, so feed regularly with nitrogen-rich fertilizer and keep the soil moist at all times. Cabbages attract pests, so be on your guard! Take preventive measures—cloches help young seedlings—and sow more than one crop successionally to ensure you have a reserve crop if all else fails. Marigolds planted nearby can be a deterrent to whiteflies, but only when they are in their strong growing phase.

Cut cabbages when the head has fully hearted up. Kale leaves can be cut as needed with pruning shears or sharp scissors.

Cabbage is delicious sliced thinly as a salad with a mayonnaise dressing, and it is equally good braised with onions, garlic, raisins, and juniper berries and served as an accompaniment to boiled ham. For the latter, cook the vegetables in a little butter, add the other ingredients and some seasoning, along with a few tablespoons of water, and simmer gently until tender. Add chopped parsley just before serving.

BELOW, FROM LEFT TO RIGHT
Cabbage 'January King,' 'Dwarf Green Curled' kale, and young cabbages are planted with French marigolds in order to deter whiteflies.

HARVESTING

CABBAGE FOR THE TABLE

raphanus sativus

Radishes can be be grown as a summer or winter crop. The summer-harvested radishes are small and mature fast. The winter radishes are larger. Both kinds can be either round (about 1 in. in diameter) or cylindrical (about 2 in. or longer). The skin can be red or white, or even yellow or black in some varieties, but the flesh is white, peppery, and crisp. The "hot" flavor becomes more intense if the radishes are not watered frequently. Radishes are a good source of vitamin C and potassium.

VARIETIES

There are many to choose from: **summer radishes** 'Cherry Belle Round': red skin; 'French Breakfast': long, with red skin and white tips; 'Scarlet Globe': round, with red skin; 'White Icicle': long, with white skin. **winter radishes** 'China Rose': long, with red skin; 'Noir de Paris': long, with brown skin.

CONTAINER SIZE

Almost any container will take a few radishes, even a small pot or window box. Alternatively, because they grow quickly, they can share a larger container with later-maturing vegetables like beans.

CULTIVATION

Sow summer radishes from spring onward, in succession, to ensure a regular supply for salads. Sow winter radishes in midsummer. Spring-sown radishes can be grown in full sun, but summer-sown radishes for winter use are best grown in partial shade. You need to sow radishes at an even depth of about ½ in. Thin summer radishes to 3 in. apart, winter radishes to 4 in. apart, and use the thinnings in salads. (Radishes do not transplant well.) As radishes grow quickly, they can become leggy if too closely spaced. In that event, the roots may fail to develop properly, or some will and others won't. If the compost has too much nitrogen, you will get too much leaf at the expense of the root. Because they mature fast, they are usually free from pests and disease, although cabbage root flies and flea beetles can be a problem.

The crop will be ready within four to eight weeks of sowing, depending on the variety.

HARVESTING

Radishes are delicious served as a simple starter on their own, particularly when they are very fresh and neither too hot nor too dry. Wash the radishes well, twist off the leaves, and chill them in the refrigerator for an hour. Serve whole with cold, unsalted butter and very fresh French bread. Alternatively, serve sliced with other salad ingredients, such as carrots, apples, and watercress.

RADISHES FOR THE TABLE

FAR LEFT 'French Breakfast' radishes have long, red-and-white-skinned, cylindrical roots, which make good use of container space.

LEFT 'Scarlet Globe' round, red-skinned radishes have good flavor.

peas

pisum sativum

'Pilot': a main-crop pea which crops well and is therefore a good choice for container growing.

This relatively fast-growing annual is a valuable source of vitamins C and B1, as well as valuable phytochemicals and folic acid. When growing them in the open, you have the choice of first or second earlies, or main-crop peas. For container growing, where space is limited, you may prefer snow or sugar snap peas, which have greater flavor and the bonus of being able to eat both the pod and the peas. Peas are natural climbers, using small leaf petioles to do so. You will need to create a support system for them, such as bamboo canes with wires and/or strings stretched horizontally between the canes.

VARIETIES

'Meteor': a first early pea; 'Sugar Snap': a high-yielding, taller-growing pea with good flavor: 'Sugar Rae': a snap pea; not as productive as 'Sugar Snap' but grows less tall; 'Dwarf Gray Sugar': a snow pea, with a dwarf habit and a good yield; 'Early Onward': a first early pea; 'Pilot': a main-crop pea with a good cropping period; 'Purple Podded': a main-crop pea with decorative, purple pods.

CONTAINER SIZE

You can grow approximately eight pea plants in a 12-in. container. To get a good crop, plant in either two containers of this size or one larger container roughly 18 in. in diameter.

CULTIVATION

Sow first early peas indoors in midspring, ¾ in. deep in small pots. You can continue to sow outdoors at intervals in late spring and early summer, provided you sow a mildew-resistant variety in summer. It is worth sowing more than once, since peas can succumb to a variety of

problems (see below). Once the peas have reached roughly 3 in. in height, they can be planted out, provided all danger of frosts has passed, or covered with a cloche if the weather turns cold. Harden off the young plants (see page 20), transplant them into their full-sized container, and provide a support system, such as a cone of canes tied into a wigwam shape. You can invent all manner of supports, from turkey wire to netting, but the peas will need lateral and vertical supports at fairly regular intervals, to which the small tendrils can cling. Keep them well watered and feed them once a month with a general organic fertilizer.

Unfortunately, peas can attract both pests and diseases. Birds and mice should be less of a problem when gardening in containers, particularly on a balcony. String brightly colored foil above plants to scare off birds. Damping-off diseases can attack early sowings, and pea moths may attack later ones.

HARVESTING

Remove the entire pod for sugar snap and snow peas, snipping it off at the stem. They should be ready eleven weeks after sowing. Shelling peas will be ready twelve to sixteen weeks after sowing. They should be harvested as soon as the pods bulge noticeably. If you leave them too long, the peas may become hard and dry.

PEAS FOR THE TABLE

Snow peas are delicious. To enjoy them at their best, stir-fry them. Heat a little oil in a wok, add the snow peas with a small amount of grated fresh ginger and shredded garlic, and stir briskly for a few minutes until tender but still crisp.

beans

Of all the vegetables you can grow, beans are among the most deserving of your precious space. They are an excellent source of protein, especially if you are vegetarian, and generally they are easy plants to grow. From a container gardener's point of view, the best beans to grow are those eaten fresh, either the whole pod or the beans within. Pole, French, and fava beans are the best for this purpose. Other beans in the family are soy and lima beans, which are normally dried, and peanuts. Mung beans can be eaten as sprouts and are extremely nutritious, so they are certainly worth growing. All you need to do is soak the beans overnight in warm water, rinse them thoroughly, and then spread them on a damp cloth. Cover with plastic wrap and brown paper. Between six to nine days later, the sprouts will be a couple of inches long and ready to use.

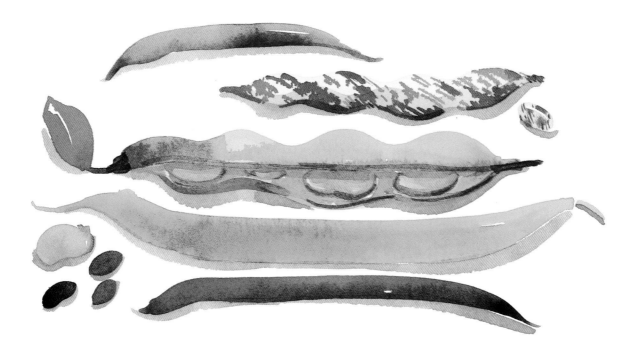

p o l e   b e a n s

phaseolus coccineus

Perennials grown as annuals in cooler climates, pole beans are useful if your garden is slightly shady, as they will grow better in less-sunny conditions than other beans. They grow on vines that will reach up to 14 ft. if allowed to do so and need a strong support system—you can pinch out the tops when several trusses of flowers have formed to keep them to more manageable proportions. One of the great advantages of growing pole beans is that they produce a mass of attractive flowers, which are also edible.

VARIETIES   There are a number of good varieties, including 'Desiree': stringless beans, with good flavor and white flowers; 'Hammond Dwarf Scarlet': a bush variety that needs no support; 'Painted Lady': not the best beans but singularly pretty red and white flowers; 'Scarlet Runner': a very popular bean with bright scarlet flowers, and a heavy cropper, with a very good flavor.

CULTIVATION   Sow the seeds—the beans themselves—indoors roughly two or three weeks before the usual last frosts in your area. Sow each seed about 2 in. deep. Transplant them into their permanent container once all danger of frost has passed. Plant roughly four or five beans to a container approximately 12 in. in diameter. Insert a long—at least 5 ft.—cane at each station and tie the tops together to form a wigwam effect. Alternatively, plant the beans in a long trough and support them using strings tied to a wall. The beans will twine themselves around the supports. If they outgrow the structure and you already have several flower trusses on each plant, pinch out the growing tip to keep them under control.

Keep the compost moist at all times, because if you forget to water, the beans will become tough and stringy. Feed once every two weeks with a general organic fertilizer once the beans start to form.

Slugs and snails may attack the young plants, so go out at night with a flashlight and remove them before they do any damage. Aphids will also attack young shoots, so spray the plants with insecticidal soap at the first signs of an attack.

HARVESTING

Pick the beans regularly when they are small (about fifteen weeks after sowing). Hold the main stem in one hand while you pull each bean off with the other, otherwise you may inadvertently tug the whole plant out. Pole beans taste better and are much more tender when they are young. Regular picking will encourage more bean pods to form. If you grow more than you can eat, you can freeze them, though they do become slightly flabby. Whole snap beans freeze much better.

snap beans

phaseolus vulgaris

Although you can eat the seeds of snap or French beans, they are really only worth growing in containers for their fresh, young pods, which are eaten whole. They come in bush (dwarf) and climbing forms. Both are suitable for containers. They need more sunshine than runner beans and the climbing forms will need similar supports, such as a wigwam or bamboo canes.

VARIETIES

Different varieties have variously shaped—round or flat—and colored pods (green, gold, or purple). 'Blue Lake': a round, green climbing bean,

which produces a good crop and can also be dried as haricots; 'The Prince': a dwarf, flat bean; 'Rocdor Yellow Wax': a yellow-podded bush bean with good flavor; 'Royal Burgundy Purple Red': a purple-podded dwarf bean. The pods turn green when cooked.

Climbing snap beans, such as 'Cobra,' need a similar support structure to pole beans, although they do not grow as tall.

You can get a crop of beans from even smallish containers—10 in. in diameter—which will allow between six and eight beans per pot.

CONTAINER SIZE

See pole beans (see page 56).

CULTIVATION

Unlike pole beans, snap beans will freeze well if you have surplus crop. Remember to blanch them for a minute or so in boiling water before freezing them.

HARVESTING

fava beans
vicia faba

Fava beans are hardy and can be overwintered if you wish. They are extremely nutritious and, along with potatoes, have long been a staple peasant crop. However, not everyone likes them. Eating them while they are still very young is the secret. Once they are older, the skin encasing the individual beans becomes tough and bitter.

You can plant the seeds in either fall or spring. Fall sowing means they get off to an early start and often avoid attacks of blackflies, for which the young shoots are a great attraction.

There are dwarf bush beans (up to 12 in. tall), as well as the standard-sized ones which grow to about 4 ft. tall. In addition, there are both long-podded and short-podded beans. The short-podded ones are thought to have the best flavor. 'Green Windsor': a short-podded variety with

VARIETIES

green beans; 'White Windsor': similar, but with white beans; 'The Sutton': a dwarf bush bean; 'Bonny Lad': another dwarf bean, but slightly taller—around 15 in.—than 'The Sutton.'

CONTAINER SIZE   Grow in a 10-in.-diameter container.

CULTIVATION   Sow the beans in either late fall or early spring, about 2 in. deep and about 4 in. apart in a container with a good depth of compost—at least 8 in. On a windy site, give the young plants some support as they grow—put in a few canes around the perimeter of the pot and tie them with string about 6 in. up. Keep well watered.

Fava beans are sometimes vulnerable to fungus—which is often called "chocolate spot" because of the accompanying discoloration—for which there is no remedy. Pull up the plants and throw them away—don't compost them! Don't go for fall sowing if this happens to your crop because fall-sown plants are more vulnerable. Aphids are the other possible problem; spray with insecticidal soap or simply rub them off with your fingers. If the beans are well grown when the attack occurs, pinch out the tips, which are the major attraction.

HARVESTING   Pick when the pods are still relatively small (no more than 6 in. long). Fall- or early-spring-sown varieties will be ready from early summer onward. If you pick them when they are small (around 3 in.), you can eat both the pod and the bean, as you would snow peas. To harvest beans, hold the stem with one hand and pick the beans with the other to avoid pulling up the whole plant.

beans in garlic

Cook the beans in lightly salted water until just tender. Then melt a small pat of butter in the pan, stir in the garlic and seasoning, and toss the beans in it for about a minute before serving.

1½ cups snap beans or shelled fava beans

pat of butter

2 cloves of garlic, crushed

seasoning

tagliatelle with baby zucchini, baby fava beans, and snow peas

Heat the olive oil in a heavy-based frying pan, and fry the garlic until golden. Add the tagliatelle to a pan of boiling salted water and cook for three to four minutes. Add the vegetables to the garlic and cook for a few more minutes until barely soft. Add the cream and lemon juice and allow to warm. Drain the tagliatelle, tip the vegetables into the center, and sprinkle with the grated Parmesan and torn basil. Serve with arugula salad.

3 tbsp. olive oil

3 cloves of garlic, crushed

3 cups fresh tagliatelle

handful each of baby zucchini, sliced, shelled fava beans, and snow peas

½ cup cream

2 tbsp. lemon juice

4 tbsp. grated Parmesan, plus shave a few extra long curls

basil, to taste

S A L A D
L E A V E S

All kinds of leaves make interesting salad ingredients, so try to grow as wide a range as possible. They are sometimes called "salad greens," but this name is something of a misnomer, since there is now an increasingly wide range of interesting colors to add to the panoply of edible leaves. Apart from their nutritional content, salads of more varied leaves add zest to any meal and are a useful source of vitamin C, as well as A and B. For those raised on bland iceberg lettuce and tomato salads, it can be a bit challenging to start eating radish leaves and vegetable thinnings. But once converted, you will not look back!

With limited space in which to grow salad leaves, it pays to plant successionally, so that as one crop finishes, another is ready for the table. With careful planning, and the use of a cloche or two, you should be able to enjoy fresh leaves all year round.

The staple of any salad is nearly always lettuce, in one form or another, so this makes a good place to start.

Young 'Little Gem' romaine lettuce grown in a box. As they mature rapidly—in a matter of a few weeks—you can grow them in any container, such as this fruit basket.

lettuces

lactuca sativa

Lettuces are extremely varied in taste, texture, appearance, and flavor. From a grower's point of view, they are grouped into several major categories. In one group are the cabbage-type lettuces that form a round heart and can be either soft-leaved (butterhead) or crisp (crisp-head). In another is the romaine lettuce, which has an elongated appearance with crispy leaves and heart. There is an intermediate group, which is a cross between these two types. Another group is the loose-leafed lettuces that do not form a heart but have frilly leaves, which are plucked as needed.

BELOW, FROM LEFT TO RIGHT
'Continuity,' a butterhead lettuce, 'Paris Island,' a romaine type, and 'Valdarz,' a loose-leafed lettuce.

You can grow lettuce in containers as small as 6 in. in diameter, one to a pot. Alternatively, plant a row of them in a window box. You can also interplant them among taller vegetables, making good use of available container space.

There is a wide range of lettuce varieties to choose from, and it is worth growing several different types, as well as ensuring that you have a continual supply over a long season.

early-spring sowings   'Little Gem': romaine; 'Tom Thumb': butterhead; 'Ithaca': crisp-head.

later sowings   (slow-to-bolt varieties) 'Buttercrunch': romaine/butterhead cross; 'Webb's Wonderful': crisp-head; 'Salad Bowl': loose leaf.

fall sowings   'Winter Density': romaine; 'Brune d'Hiver': butterhead; 'Marvel of Four Seasons': loose leaf.

Although lettuces naturally mature in the summer, new varieties have been bred that will overwinter ready for an early crop the following summer. Sow the seeds of all lettuce thickly and cover with a fine layer of potting compost. Thin them once they are 2 in. tall. Make the first sowings in early spring indoors and plant out under cloches. Make successional sowings outdoors throughout the spring and summer. Winter-hardy lettuce can be sown in the fall and will be ready early the next summer. Water lettuce copiously and frequently. Feed once a month. Lettuce are generally free of disease, but they are susceptible to slug and snail damage.

If you are planting "cut-and-come-again" lettuce, sow the seeds about 1 in. apart in all directions—do not thin—and cut off the leaves at the base when they are about 4 in. high. Romaine lettuces, which usually take longer to mature than other types of lettuce, do well grown in this way.

Either cut individual leaves once they are a few inches tall, as you need them, or harvest whole heads approximately ten weeks after sowing.

other salad leaves

There are two kinds of Chinese cabbage: one that forms a head and another that doesn't. The latter type, known as "bok choy," is the best to grow, as it has pale, crunchy leaves, which are good for stir-fries. Different cultivars vary in height from just 4 in. to almost 2 ft., but the dwarf-growing ones make good container plants. Sow the seeds under cover in midspring or outdoors in late spring. Later sowings will be inclined to bolt. You can cut the seedlings four to five weeks after sowing as a cut-and-come-again crop. They need copious watering. Harvest whole heads ten weeks after sowing. They are subject to the same range of pests and diseases as ordinary cabbages (see page 48). Two bolt-resistant cultivars are 'Chingensai,' which has green stems, and 'Joi Choi,' which has white stems.

chinese cabbage
brassica rapa **var** *chinensis*

The flat-leaved chicories (*C. intybus*) and endive, the curly leaved form (*C. endivia*), can be used in salads or as a cooked vegetable. The leaves are grown for salads, and the roots are cooked. There are many different forms and colors. The flowers, a pretty blue, are edible and can also be used in salads (see pages 132–5). The leaves are bitter and will normally need blanching once they are full size to make them palatable, but you can pick the young leaves for salads. Grow the red-leaved chicories (often labeled on seed packets as "radicchio," the Italian name for chicory) to add color to your salads. Sow the seeds just after the last frosts have passed and carry on sowing successively every couple of weeks. Cut the leaves when they are about 3 in. tall. Water well and feed occasionally to encourage more leaves to grow.

chicory
cichorium spp.

Bok choy, one of many different types of Chinese greens, is a useful, easy-to-grow, leafy vegetable with a crunchy texture. It is good for both stir-fries and salads.

arugula
eruca sativa

This hot and spicy salad vegetable is a very fast-growing salad crop, which will quickly bolt in hot weather. Sow seeds in early spring to prevent this or make successional sowings in partial shade. It does well interplanted with larger vegetables to save space. Sow the seeds fairly thickly on the surface of the compost and keep moist to prevent bolting. If you succeed in keeping the container moist at all times, you can use it as a cut-and-come-again crop; it will resprout a couple of times. If a pot does run to seed, you can save the seeds for the following year's supply.

Arugula, one of the fastest-growing and easiest salad crops to grow, adds spice to blander- tasting salad leaves.

These grow extremely easily, even on damp cardboard or blotting paper, and are particularly good for adding flavor to sandwiches or egg dishes. Sow the seeds thickly and evenly in wide-diameter, fairly shallow containers on premoistened compost, but do not cover with soil. Cover the top of the container to encourage germination and move into the light once the seedlings are roughly 1 in. high. Cut when 2 in. tall. Mustard germinates more quickly than cress, so if you want both together, sow the mustard a few days after the cress. Let one pot run to seed and collect the seeds for next year's crop.

mustard and cress
sinapsis alba

Particularly useful on account of its hardiness, corn salad (sometimes known as "lamb's lettuce") has mild-flavored, small, rounded leaves. A small plant, growing to no more than 6 in. all around, it can be planted with taller vegetables. It is relatively slow growing. Sow it in early summer for a fall or winter crop—it will take roughly three months to mature—or use it sooner as a cut-and-come-again crop. Corn salad will overwinter in relatively mild climates, but a cloche will improve the leaf texture. 'Verte de Cambrai' and 'Verte d'Etapes' are both very hardy cultivars.

corn salad
valerianella locusta

If you opt for the cut-and-come-again method of harvesting salad vegetables, you will be able to pick salad leaves over a long season. Make sure when you wash them that you dry them thoroughly, as wet lettuce and dressing do not go well together. Mix the ingredients for whatever dressing you prefer (see page 138) and toss the salad in the dressing just before serving.

SALAD LEAVES FOR THE TABLE

tomatoes

lycopersicon esculentum

OPPOSITE ABOVE   Mixed tomatoes: 'Auriga,' 'Pink Debut,' golden cherry tomatoes, and green 'Zebra.'

OPPOSITE BELOW   Sweet-flavored 'Rose de Berne' tomatoes.

The tomato, a tender perennial, is native to South America and was introduced into Europe in the sixteenth century. In their natural habitat, tomato plants grow very vigorously and fruit copiously, but in colder climates, you may have to coax them into fruiting well if there are inadequate levels of sunshine after the plants have set fruits. In cold or wet areas, try growing them under a cloche or bringing them indoors to a conservatory or a position in front of a sunny window. Nonetheless, the tomato is one of the best crops to grow in containers, producing abundant supplies from relatively little space, thanks to the plant's climbing habit.

Tomatoes are packed with vitamins and are rich in phytochemicals. Recent research indicates that tomatoes—even when cooked—have great health benefits, including cancer-fighting properties.

VARIETIES

There are three principal types to grow: tall, bush, or dwarf. The tall types need training up strings or poles, the bush types will sprawl (and can even be grown in a hanging basket), and the dwarf types form miniature bushes, ideal for very tiny spaces but with smaller yields.

There is a wealth of choice, from huge beefsteak tomatoes to tiny cherry ones, in a splendid range of colors, including yellows, pinks, white, and striped. Of the varieties of size and type popularly available, the following are all worth growing: 'Beefmaster' (beefsteak type), 'Marmande,' 'Gardener's Delight,' and 'Sweet 100.'

CONTAINER SIZE

Containers should be at least 10 in. in diameter and ideally 12 in. deep for each plant. If you prefer, use a growing bag. One large growing bag will take three tomato plants—ample for a two-person household. A family of four might need six plants in two growing bags.

CULTIVATION

Sow three seeds in a small pot in the gentle heat of midspring. Germination will take about a week. Thin them down to one seed per pot once they reach the three-leaf stage. Transplant them when they are about 6 in. tall into the growing bag once any danger of frost is past (about six to eight weeks after sowing). Alternatively, you can buy young plants grown in individual pots. Give tall tomatoes a supporting cane that is at least 3 ft. high.

As the tomato plant grows, tie the main stem to the cane loosely, taking care not to damage it. You will need to "stop" the plant once four or five trusses have appeared (see below) and remove surplus leaves that grow between the side shoots and the main stem.

1

2

PINCHING OUT
1 Pinch out the non–flower-bearing side shoots and the basal growths at the point at which the trusses start to form. Tomato plants need warm roots, and too much foliage diverts the energy of the plant, which should be directed into flowering and fruiting.

2 In high summer, when there are four or five trusses of fruits on the plant, pinch out the growing point (the uppermost growth).

Tomatoes need a sunny spot to fruit well. Tall-growing varieties, such as this cherry tomato, should be tied in to a good support system.

Tomatoes in containers need frequent watering, at least a couple of times a week and more often in hot weather or if grown under glass. Less frequent watering will result in tomatoes with good flavor but very tough skins. Feed the plants with an organic tea (see page 23) once every couple of weeks until the fruits ripen.

Tomatoes are relatively trouble free, but you might find it worthwhile to plant French marigolds around the base: they look attractive and help to deter whiteflies. Put mulch around the base to protect the plants from slugs and to conserve moisture.

HARVESTING

The tomatoes should be ready to pick in late summer. Any that are still green in early fall can be taken off the plant, wrapped in paper, and stored in a dark drawer—make sure the tomatoes are in good condition at this point or you will end up with a drawer full of mold—or place them out on a plate. Placing one ripe tomato in a bowl of green ones will help them complete the ripening process more quickly, as ripe tomatoes give off a chemical that encourages the process in neighboring fruits. Failing that, green tomatoes make excellent chutney (see page 138).

TOMATOES FOR THE TABLE

To get the maximum benefit from tomatoes and to appreciate their flavor, pick them on a sunny day and eat them raw, straight from the plant. Do not, whatever you do, refrigerate them if you plan to use them in salads, as chilling destroys their flavor. This is particularly true of the smaller tomatoes, such as the cherry types. The bigger beefsteak tomatoes can either be used for salads or stuffed and baked. Use slightly overripe tomatoes for tomato and basil soup (see basic soup recipe, page 140), tomato and pepper pasta sauce (see page 85), or with other vegetables for ratatouille.

tomato and goat cheese bruschetta

Halve the tomatoes and roast them in a warm oven for fifteen minutes. Slice the baguette and cook on a rack in the oven for the last ten minutes. Spread the tomatoes, goat cheese, garlic, and basil leaves on the slices. Drizzle with olive oil and serve warm.

1 cup cherry tomatoes
½ baguette
medium goat cheese, roughly cubed
2 cloves garlic, finely chopped
Small handful of torn basil leaves
3 tbsp. olive oil

mozzarella and tomato salad

Use good-quality mozzarella for this (buffalo mozzarella, if preferred). Slice the tomatoes and mozzarella into rings. Lay them on a plate. Either chop the garlic finely or crush it in a garlic crusher. Sprinkle the garlic and basil over the tomatoes. Drizzle with olive oil and lemon juice. Season to taste and garnish with a few olives. Do not refrigerate this salad; it should be served at room temperature, ideally with homemade wheat bread.

1½ cups tomatoes
1½ cups mozzarella cheese
2 large cloves of garlic
1 tbsp. fresh basil, torn
2 tbsp. olive oil
1 tbsp. lemon juice
seasoning
1 tbsp. black olives

variation
The Portuguese make a similar tomato salad, substituting sliced onions (red onions are ideal, being fairly sweet) in place of the mozzarella, and cilantro for the basil.

cucumbers

cucumis sativus

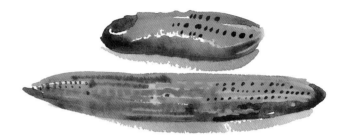

Cucumbers are tender perennials; they come from tropical parts of the world, where they make tremendous growth in a very short space of time. Although the smooth-skinned cucumbers cannot be grown outside in temperate climates, the rougher-skinned or ridged cucumbers will do extremely well. Cucumbers provide a good source of vitamins A and C, and potassium. Like other tender vegetables, they are grown in late spring to summer and fruit from midsummer onward. They need a warm, sunny spot, with shelter from cold winds. A sheet of glass behind the support will help protect the crop and increase the warmth. Gherkins are grown in precisely the same way as cucumbers, but they take up less space and are therefore ideal for containers. Pick them when they are roughly 2 in. long.

VARIETIES
There are a few good cucumbers to choose from, including round ones, as well as the usual long cucumbers.
long cucumber 'Nadir,' 'Baton Vert,' 'Burpee,' 'Patio Pik' (ideal for containers), 'Long Green Ridge.'
round cucumbers 'Marion.'
gherkins 'Bestal,' 'Hokus,' 'Vento Pickling."

CONTAINER SIZE
You can grow three cucumbers in a standard-sized growing bag or one per pot in a 12-in.-deep container. Unless you have a large and

hungry family with a passion for cucumbers, one or two plants will be more than adequate for your needs. The best solution is to stagger the planting by a couple of weeks so that your entire crop does not fruit at the same time.

CULTIVATION

If you sow the seeds in midspring under cover, you can put the plants out in early summer after all danger of frost has passed. Sow the large, flat seeds two to a small pot, 3 in. in diameter, and remove the weaker seedling. Harden the young plants off gradually (see page 20) before planting up in a growing bag or larger container. Alternatively, sow the seeds outside in early summer, one per pot, with a cloche over the jar to speed growth and protect the emergent seedlings from slugs.

TRANSPLANTING CUCUMBERS

1 Cucumbers dislike firm soil and being transplanted. Plant two seeds on edge in each pot.

2 When you transplant them, up-end the small pot and transfer the entire contents to a larger pot with a minimum of root disturbance.

1

2

The cucumber plants will need to be supported on canes or strings in the same way as tomato plants (see page 72) and will make even more vigorous growth. Pinch out the growing point in the same way once there are half a dozen leaves per shoot, to encourage the side shoots to fruit. Once the fruits start to form, provide a high-potash feed every two weeks.

Unsurprisingly, as they are made up mostly of water, cucumbers need frequent watering. Keep the soil moist, without waterlogging it. If you fail to water adequately, you will have small, rather tough cucumbers with very bitter skins—if you get any at all.

Cucumber mosaic virus, which presents itself as yellowish mottling on the leaves, can be a problem about which you can do nothing except destroy the plants. Keep cucumbers away from other members of the *Cucurbitaceae* family, as they are all prone to the disease. If the plants are attacked by red spider mites—more likely if they are grown under glass—the foliage becomes rust colored. If you look very carefully, you will see the tiny insects on the undersides of leaves. Frequent misting with water will help prevent attacks.

HARVESTING

Pick the cucumbers when they are still fairly small—about 6 in. long. They will be ready between eight and ten weeks after planting. Twist the stalk to remove them from the plant.

CUCUMBERS FOR THE TABLE

Homegrown cucumbers make delicious sandwiches. Potato and cucumber salad is also good. Scrape some potatoes, boil them until they are just tender, and cut them into cubes. Peel and cube a cucumber. Dress with homemade mayonnaise thinned with cream, and garnish with chopped parsley.

RIGHT AND FAR RIGHT Outdoor cucumbers are not as large as the ones that you can buy in the stores, but they taste better and are surprisingly easy to grow. The flowers (right) make a pretty addition to a salad. Cucumbers are ready for harvesting (far right).

z u c c h i n i

cucurbita pepo

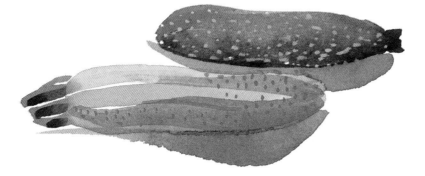

Zucchini are simply immature squash. They can be found in a marvelous range of colors, shapes, and sizes, including green, yellow, white, striped, long, round, or flat. They are a good source of vitamins A and C, calcium, and iron. There are both bush and trailing forms. The latter are ideal for small spaces, because they can be trained vertically up poles or wires, thereby taking up minimal precious ground space. Because winter squash require more space and have less flavor, they are less suitable for container growing than the smaller zucchini.

VARIETIES

How much time do you have? Choosing is likely to be the hardest part, so try a few different varieties each year to see which gives you the most pleasure. The odder ones will certainly impress your friends, although there will not be much to choose between them taste-wise.
bush types 'Early Gem,' 'Dark Green Zucchini,' 'Diamante,' 'Gold Rush.'
trailing 'Little Gem' (round fruits), 'Long Green Trailing.'

CONTAINER SIZE

Plant them in pots 12 in. in diameter and 12 in. deep, or plant three plants to a standard growing bag.

Sow the seeds, which are large and flat, on edge, two to a 3-in. pot in midspring. Plant out after the last frosts in large containers. Cover young plants with a cloche to protect them from slugs.

Water generously at all times. Support the trailing types on strings or poles, tying in as necessary to help them climb. Pinch out the leading shoots once the plants reach several feet. When flowers start to form, feed with liquid feed once every two weeks or so. The plant will produce both male and female flowers, the latter bearing the fruits.

If no fruits set—cold weather can stop insect activity and natural pollination—you may need to hand pollinate. The female flower has a tiny thickened section of stem just behind the flower. Pick a male flower, remove the petals, and brush the male organ against the center of the female flowers as carefully as you can.

As with other members of the *Cucurbitaceae* family, red spider mites and the mosaic virus cause problems. Keep spraying plants with water to control red spider mites and burn any affected by mosaic virus.

Pick the zucchini as soon as they are about 4 in. long and keep picking regularly unless you want marrows. The first fruits will form roughly ten to twelve weeks after planting.

You can eat very small zucchini raw, sliced in salads. Slightly larger ones are best lightly cooked. One of the best ways to cook them is to slice them lengthwise fairly thinly, and cook them very briefly in salted boiling water. Drain and then fry them in olive oil with crushed garlic and parsley for a few minutes until brown. Larger ones can be baked in the oven with sliced tomatoes. Slice the zucchini and tomatoes in rings and layer them in a greased ovenproof dish, dot with butter, cover with breadcrumbs and fresh mixed herbs, and bake for about twenty minutes in a 400°F oven.

Harvest the zucchini once they reach 4–6 in. in length. If you keep picking, you will encourage more to form.

peppers

capsicum spp.

OPPOSITE ABOVE 'Bell Boy' and 'Sweet Banana' peppers.

OPPOSITE BELOW 'Cayenne Long Slim' chilies. The red ones are simply riper versions of the green ones.

These tender perennials are grown as annuals in cooler climates. They are an excellent source of both vitamin C and phytochemicals, and they also contain a good quantity of vitamin A, potassium, and iron. Peppers vary in "hotness," depending on the type grown. You may choose to grow the very hot chili peppers for decoration, as much as for flavor; the sweet peppers, which are milder, are used in a wide range of dishes.

VARIETIES

sweet peppers 'Aussie Red': a large-fruiting pepper, maturing to red; 'Hungarian': a similarly large-fruiting green pepper, also maturing to red; 'Chocolate': dark brownish-purple fruits; 'Purple Beauty': deep purplish-black fruit; 'Mandy': virus-resistant, green fruits, maturing to red; 'Hero': a good choice for containers as it is virus-resistant and tolerates low temperatures.

chilies 'Cayenne Long Slim': attractive, slender cayenne-type; 'Hungarian Yellow Wax': hot, yellow fruits.

CONTAINER SIZE

Plant one to each 8-in.-diameter pot.

CULTIVATION

Make no mistake, peppers are not the easiest crop to grow, in or out of containers in cooler climates. However, they are great fun and worth a try, although insufficient sun may keep them from ripening. You can start

them off in small seed pots or blocks indoors (three seeds to a small pot or block) about two months before the predicted last frost dates for your area. Try to make sure that they get plenty of sunshine once they germinate. When the seedlings are growing strongly, you can thin them down to the strongest in each pot—don't pull them out, simply cut them off at the stem base to prevent disturbing the roots of the remaining plant. Then harden them off (see page 20), once all danger of frost has passed, for a week before planting out. Hot chili peppers will not need as much room as sweet ones.

Pinch out the plant tops once they reach 6 in. high to encourage bushy growth with lots of side shoots. Keep peppers well watered. Lack of water produces a fiery taste and often a bitter flavor. Keep them sheltered from winds, and in very hot weather, provide them with partial shade. Textbooks often tell you to allow only four to six peppers per plant, but most of us are lucky to get four!

Once the fruits start swelling, apply a high-potash liquid feed once every two weeks. If the peppers are developing late in the season, move the containers indoors to a warm windowsill.

If you are growing both hot and sweet peppers, they may cross-pollinate, giving you some surprise flavors!

Aphids, red spider mites (primarily indoors), whiteflies, and caterpillars can all cause problems. Spraying the leaves with water from time to time will help prevent aphids and red spider mites. Keep an eye out for pests, removing them by hand when spotted. Mosaic virus—which also attacks eggplants and cucumbers—can be a major problem, so try to buy virus-resistant cultivars.

HARVESTING   Keep picking peppers and chilies to encourage new fruits to form.

vegetable pasta sauce

Peel and slice the onions finely and cook in preheated pan with the oil until just soft. Deseed and slice the peppers and deseed and finely chop the chili, and add to the onions. Cook for a few minutes and then add the other ingredients. Cook for long enough for the ingredients to become soft, but not mushy, and the sauce to have thickened slightly—about ten minutes. You can add black olives, capers, and/or anchovies to this sauce, if desired, just before you serve it. You can also add an eggplant, cut into small cubes, just after the onions to give the sauce a more meaty content. Serve with plenty of grated Parmesan cheese.

2 onions

2 tbsp. olive oil

2 peppers

1 small chili

6 tomatoes, skinned and quartered

1 can tomatoes

1 tsp. tomato concentrate

2 tbsp. mixed parsley, basil, marjoram, and thyme, chopped

scant ½ cup chicken stock

seasoning

roasted vegetables

These make an excellent accompaniment to roasted or grilled meat or fish. You can vary the vegetables and quantities according to what is in season.

Heat the oven to 425°F. Peel the onions. Chop the other vegetables into quarters or roughly 2-in. chunks. Brush a roasting pan with some of the olive oil and spread the vegetables on the base. Season to taste. Brush with the remaining oil, sprinkle with the breadcrumbs and herbs, and roast for approximately thirty minutes until softened and starting to char slightly. Sprinkle with flakes of Parmesan cheese.

2 cups onions, peppers, tomatoes, zucchini, and eggplant

3 tbsp. olive oil

3 tbsp. breadcrumbs

3 tbsp. mixed fresh herbs

2 tbsp. Parmesan cheese, flaked

seasoning

variation
If you wish, you can add root vegetables to the dish, but remember that they take longer to cook, so put them in fifteen minutes before the other ingredients.

eggplants
solanum melongena

Although we are now familiar with purple-fruited eggplants, you can find white, yellow, and green ones, too, and a range of curious shapes and sizes. Eggplants need warm temperatures and a long growing season to bear fruit, so if you want to try them, you need to sow the seeds early. If you succeed in growing them, eggplants are a good source of vitamin C, iron, and fiber. They are also a great talking point! If you have trouble growing them outdoors, bring the pot indoors onto a sunny window ledge. Allow roughly twenty weeks between sowing and harvesting.

Eggplants will usually crop fairly heavily if the conditions are right, but they need shelter and sunshine to fruit well.

VARIETIES

'Long Purple': an old-fashioned favorite that has stood the test of time; 'Black Beauty': large purple fruits; 'Snowy': long white fruit; 'Kermit': green-and-white fruits, unusual round shape.

CONTAINER SIZE

Plant one plant in each 8-in.-diameter pot or three plants to a standard-sized growing bag.

CULTIVATION

Eggplant seeds can be difficult to germinate, and it helps to soak them first to soften the hard outer casing. They can take between two and three weeks to germinate. Sow three seeds to a pot in midspring under cover and thin to the strongest seedling when these reach 3 in. in height. Harden off (see page 20) over a week or so. Eggplants need shelter from strong winds and will benefit from slight shade in very hot weather. A cloche or glass protection may be needed to encourage fruiting in colder climates. Keep them well watered. Stake the plant with a cane. You can encourage the plant to bush out more by pinching out the leading shoot once the plant reaches 12 in. in height. Feed regularly with a high-potash, organic fertilizer once the fruits begin to form. Should your plant produce copious quantities of fruit, reduce the number to four to encourage these to swell fully.

The main potential problems are aphids and red spider mites. Remove any aphids by hand and spray the leaves and shoots regularly with water to discourage red spider mites.

HARVESTING   Snip off any fruit regularly once they reach about 4 in. in size. Regular picking will encourage fruiting. Eggplants will keep in the refrigerator for up to two weeks.

'Black Prince' is a popular variety of eggplant and one that fruits well in cooler climates. As with all tender vegetables, protection will increase the likelihood of the fruits ripening.

beignets d'aubergine

These eggplant fritters are made with a very light batter. You can also use this batter to fry zucchini flowers. Simply mix the flour with a little seasoning and enough water to make a thin cream. Then just before using the batter, stiffly beat two egg whites and fold them into the mixture. Cut the eggplants into thin rings, dip them in the batter, and fry in deep, very hot oil for a couple of minutes. Drain on kitchen paper. Zucchini flower fritters require a very brief frying time.

4 heaping tbsp. flour
1 large or 2 small eggplants
2 egg whites
seasoning
oil for frying

eggplant with goat cheese

These make a quick, delicious lunch or dinner. Slice the eggplants into ½-in.-thick rounds and brush both sides with olive oil. Fry the eggplants on each side until just tender. Preheat the broiler to the highest temperature. Spread one side of each eggplant slice with a thick layer of the tomato paste and the crushed garlic. Slice the goat cheese into rings and put one ring on each eggplant slice. Broil the eggplant slices until the cheese melts. Sprinkle with basil, season to taste, and serve on a bed of arugula salad.

2 eggplants
2 tbsp. olive oil
sun-dried tomato paste (or similar)
2 cloves garlic, finely chopped or crushed
goat cheese
1 tbsp. torn basil leaves
seasoning

OTHER VEGETABLES

kohlrabi
brassica oleracea 'gongylodes'

This member of the cabbage family is grown for its swollen, bulblike stem, which varies in color from pale green to purple. There are fast- and slow-maturing varieties, the fastest taking about a month and a half to mature. They can be sown as late as early fall for winter supplies, otherwise sow the seeds in midspring, three to a pot, thinning to one per 8-in.-diameter container. Unlike many other vegetables, kohlrabi is relatively tolerant to drought, but will grow best if watered frequently.

turnip
brassica rapa rapifera group

This is a biennial whose roots are a rich source of vitamin C and a good source of vitamin A, folic acid, and calcium. The white or yellow roots are cooked. Although large turnips can be slightly tasteless, the French have long enjoyed very young turnips, which suit container-growing admirably. Plant the seeds in spring and thin out to 4 in. between plants once the seedlings reach 3 in. tall. If you grow them successionally from spring to early summer, you will have a constant supply from summer to fall. Use a bolt-resistant variety for later sowings and make sure you water turnips well at all times. 'Golden Ball' is a good yellow-fleshed turnip, and 'Tokyo Cross' is quick growing. Harvest once the roots are 2 in. in diameter. Turnips are not particularly prone to pests and diseases, although young seedlings may be attacked by flea beetles. Protect them with cloches to prevent attacks.

artichoke
cynara cardunculus

Whether or not you choose to eat its curiously armadillo-like flower buds, the artichoke makes a handsome feature plant in its own right, with its large, silvery leaves and attractive blue flowers. It will benefit from a

large container, at least 10 in. in diameter. It is probably best to grow artichokes by purchasing a container-grown plant or dividing an existing plant; otherwise, you will have to wait two years for the flower buds to form. For culinary purposes, harvest the flower buds in midsummer, while they are still young, cutting them from the main plant just below the base of the bud with a sharp knife. Keep picking to encourage further production.

The nutty, potato-like root of the Jerusalem artichoke is full of flavor and a valuable source of B vitamins. Jerusalem artichokes are easy and quick to grow, but are also very large. Grow them as you would potatoes, in a deep barrel, from mature roots cut into pieces and planted 3 in. deep. The plants will grow to 6 ft. tall and will make an excellent windbreak for other more tender plants. Harvest the roots in fall. Jerusalem artichokes are pest and disease free. The downside, however, is that they can cause a considerable amount of gas in your stomach!

You can make excellent mashed potatoes by cooking both Jerusalem artichokes and potatoes together until tender and then mashing them with a generous quantity of light cream. Chop in a tablespoonful of parsley, and season with salt and pepper.

artichoke, jerusalem
helianthus tuberosus

FAR LEFT Turnips are delicious if harvested young and small.

LEFT Artichokes should also be picked when young for the best flavor and texture. 'Green Globe' shown here is a popular and useful variety.

fruits

soft fruits · bush fruits ·
tree fruits · other fruits

strawberries
fragaria x ananassa

Although we often think of strawberries as having a short season, lasting for just a few weeks in midsummer, it is possible, with a little forethought and ingenuity, to enjoy a much longer strawberry season. There are several varieties of strawberries, known as "remontant" or "perpetual," which fruit later than usual, and continue to do so until late fall. You can also force summer-fruiting strawberries to ripen earlier in the season by covering them with a plastic cloche.

RIGHT 'Elsanta' is a good choice for a hanging basket, with abundant crops of small, sweet fruits.

FAR RIGHT A purpose-made strawberry pot maximizes space.

OPPOSITE 'Gorella' strawberries growing in individual terra-cotta pots on wooden staging on a narrow balcony.

Strawberries grow very well in pots and tubs of all kinds. Modern strawberry production favors growing bags on raised tables. Grown this way, they are less prone to attacks by slugs and vine weevils. You can also buy purpose-made strawberry pots, with planting pockets up the sides of the pot, or you can create one yourself out of a barrel. Drill holes roughly 3 in. in diameter up the sides, staggering them around the barrel, roughly 6 in. apart. Originating in woodland conditions, strawberries, unlike many other fruits, will tolerate partial shade but they fruit much better in full sun. After a couple of years, the plants will be exhausted, but you can pot up the runners that form each year to increase your stock.

VARIETIES

There is a wide range to choose from, from early and midseason to late-fall-fruiting crops, as well as the smaller alpine forms of strawberries (*F. vesca*), which make up for the lack of size with exceptionally sweet, full-flavored fruits. Among the best of the early and midseason strawberries are 'Florence,' 'Elsanta,' 'Elvira,' and 'Royal Sovereign.'

Late-fruiting types include 'Gorella' and 'Cambridge Late Pine.' Remontant, or perpetual, varieties, which fruit for a much longer season, include the French variety, 'Mara des Bois,' which has the flavor of a woodland strawberry with the size of a cultivated one and is an extremely heavy cropper.

CONTAINER SIZE

You can grow strawberries in small pots, about 6 in. in diameter, one plant to each pot—a single plant will produce up to 1 lb. of strawberries. Special strawberry planters allow you to grow up to twenty plants in each pot, making good use of the available space.

CULTIVATION

Buy young strawberry plants in late summer and plant them in early fall. Unless you plan to devote a lot of space to strawberries, it is probably better to plant several plants that fruit at the same time. Make sure that the plants are well watered at all times. If you grow them in a strawberry planter, take care that the lowest plants get an adequate water supply. Feed with an organic fertilizer from flowering onward. Once the fruits start to swell, watch for slugs and snails—although these tend to be less of a problem with container-grown plants—and remove them. In late summer remove any offshoots (runners) and plant them in separate pots to increase your stock of strawberries.

Birds are the greatest problem, and you may need to net your strawberry containers.

HARVESTING

Pick the fruits as soon as they redden. Strawberries do not keep well, nor do they freeze well. Eat them the day they are picked.

STRAWBERRIES FOR THE TABLE

You can use strawberries either as the main ingredient for a dessert, or if you have very few, as a decoration. They make a marvelous accompaniment to fresh lemon tart—made using the recipe for plum tart on page 121, but substituting lemons for the plums; you will need the rind and juice of two fresh lemons. Strawberry ice cream is equally delicious. Use the ice cream recipe on page 106, substituting strawberries for the main ingredient.

strawberry mille-feuilles

Unroll the phyllo pastry, cut it into neat rectangles of about 3 x 1½ in. and place on a greased cookie sheet. Cook in a very hot oven (or as directed on the package) until crisp and golden. Remove and cool on a wire rack. Beat the cream until thick. Slice the strawberries and layer the strawberries with the cream between the sheets of phyllo pastry. Dust the tops of the slices with powdered sugar and garnish each one with half a strawberry and a sprig of mint.

4 oz. phyllo pastry (store-bought)

1 cup heavy cream

2 cups strawberries

powdered sugar and mint sprigs to garnish

strawberries and lemon syllabub

The combination of strawberries with lemon always works well. You only need a few strawberries for this. If desired, you can substitute peaches for the strawberries.

Halve the strawberries and divide them evenly among four glasses, setting aside four for decoration. Whip the cream, adding the lemon juice and rind, white wine, and sugar gradually to prevent curdling. Spoon the mixture over the strawberries and decorate with a single strawberry and a sprinkling of brown sugar. Chill well before serving.

1½ cups strawberries, washed and hulled

1¼ cups heavy cream

juice and rind of 2 small lemons

½ glass sweet white wine

3 tbsp. sugar

BUSH FRUITS

There are several types of bush fruits, all of which will do well in containers. You can choose from brambles (*Rosaceae* family), such as raspberries and blackberries, or currants and gooseberries (*Grossulariaceae* family). There are hybridized raspberries, blackberries, currants, and gooseberries. Loganberries are a cross between raspberries and blackberries, with exceptionally large, wine-colored fruit, while jostaberries are a hybrid between gooseberries and black currants, with particularly large black fruits.

Even if you do not manage to get a very large crop from a single bush, there is nothing to keep you from growing several different types and then using the mixed fruits in various desserts or for making a mixed fruit jelly.

You will need to provide a suitable support framework for raspberries and blackberries, both of which are best grown against a sunny wall. Use a simple trellis system of posts and wires. The greatest yield of fruits will be obtained if you train the new canes horizontally along the wires, tying them in with string or twist ties.

If you wish, you can train your gooseberry bushes into small standards by removing the lower side shoots to create a mop head of foliage and fruits at the top.

You can get surprisingly good yields from a single fruit bush if you feed the plants with a potash-based fertilizer in early spring. A mulch of your own compost or straw around the base of the plant will help to retain moisture, and in the case of compost, feed the plants at the same time.

RIGHT Young 'Invicta' gooseberries (right) and 'Laxton's Giant' black currants (far right).

gooseberries

ribes uva-crispa

There are two kinds of gooseberries—the dessert gooseberry with large golden or reddish fruits and the small-fruited, culinary gooseberry. Both are grown in the same way, but the culinary gooseberries are more heat-tolerant and mildew-resistant. If you wish, you can grow gooseberry bushes as half-standards with a couple of feet of clear stem and underplant them with herbs.

VARIETIES

dessert gooseberries 'Early Sulphur,' 'Langley Gage,' and 'Leveller' (all yellow); 'Poorman' and 'Clark' (red).
culinary gooseberries 'Careless,' 'Jubilee,' and 'Invicta.'

CONTAINER SIZE

Plant in a container at least 12 in. in diameter and at least 12 in. deep.

CULTIVATION

Plant young gooseberry bushes in the fall. A sunny site will produce the best crop, but they will cope with partial shade. They prefer lower amounts of nitrogen and plenty of potassium and magnesium. Mulching the container with gravel or straw after planting will help to conserve moisture. Feed with a high-potash fertilizer in early spring. Once the fruits set, you need to water regularly. If you let the compost dry out and then water copiously, the fruits may burst. Prune after fruiting, taking lateral shoots back to three to five leaves—leaving leaders unpruned—and pruning to an outward-facing bud. Aphids and mildews are the main problems. Remove aphids by hand and use sulphur to control mildews.

HARVEST

Pick early gooseberries for jams or compotes and later ones for fully ripe, dessert gooseberries.

Dessert gooseberries, which are larger and sweeter than the culinary forms, are eaten raw. Those shown here are 'Langley Gage.'

currants

ribes nigrum (black currants)*, r. rubrum* (white and red currants)

Currants do well in containers, and are relatively easy to grow and maintain. They will grow to about 4 ft. tall, bearing white, red, black or gold currants, according to the type. Although currants are self-fertile, many cultivars benefit from cross-pollination, so it pays to grow more than one bush if you can. Unlike gooseberries, they like plenty of nitrogen, so feed them accordingly. With good plant management, you should obtain a good yield off just one plant, normally up to 10 lbs. per bush. Jostaberries, a cross between gooseberries and black currants, crop slightly less heavily.

VARIETIES

black currants 'Ben Sarek': a dwarf variety with lots of fruits; 'Laxton's Giant': particularly large, sweet fruits.
red currants 'Red Lake' and 'Malling Redstart': both heavy fruiting.
white currants 'White Versailles': good all-arounder; 'White Imperial': good flavor.

CONTAINER SIZE

A 12-in.-diameter container is best, although, as they are fairly shallow rooted, you could grow them in a growing bag.

CULTIVATION

Plant currant bushes in fall or winter. Black currants need to be planted deeper than red currants, with the uppermost roots about 3 in. below the surface. The roots of red currants can be about 1 in.

below the surface of the compost. Mulching the surface after planting with gravel or chipped bark will help to retain moisture. Apply high-nitrogen organic fertilizer at the start of the growing season and keep the soil moist. Cut back the leading shoots by roughly half after planting and trim the lateral shoots to a couple of buds, making the cuts above downward- and outward-facing buds. Prune lightly in subsequent years to keep an open-shaped bush. Alternatively, you can grow red and white currants as cordons, by removing all but one of the leaders and training up a stake. Aphids and mildew can be problems on currants.

Currants will be ready for picking from midsummer onward, depending on the cultivar. When you harvest them, remove a whole fruit cluster rather than the individual fruits. Currants do not keep well once picked, but they freeze extremely well.

HARVESTING

White currants have excellent flavor but tend to crop less heavily than the more ubiquitous black currants.

r a s p b e r r i e s

rubus idaea

There are two fruiting seasons for raspberries—summer and fall—so if you choose the right varieties, you can extend the raspberry season. You can also grow raspberry/blackberry hybrids, like tayberries and worcesterberries or the more commonly known boysenberries and loganberries.

VARIETIES
There are early-, mid-, and late-summer raspberries, and fall-fruiting ones, as well.

summer fruiting 'Boyne': early season, red fruits; 'Algonquin': midseason, red fruits; 'Haida': late season, red fruits.

autumn fruiting 'Autumn Bliss': early fall, large fruits; 'Ruby': late fall, very large fruits.

CONTAINER SIZE
Plant two or three plants in a container about 12 in. across. For a good crop, have at least two such containers.

CULTIVATION
Plant young raspberry plants in late fall or early spring in a fairly alkaline growing medium and set any bareroot plants about 2 in. deeper than they were in the nursery. Let the roots spread out. Cut off the canes to just above ground level after planting, as this will help prevent diseases. Give raspberries a good dose of compost or organic fertilizer in early spring. Keep well watered during the growing season. Provide a support system of trellising. Summer-fruiting raspberries are pruned after fruiting in early fall by cutting off fruiting canes to ground level; fall-fruiting canes are pruned in early spring. Although they can fall prey to pests and

diseases, they are usually easy to grow. If raspberry beetles are a problem, spray with derris. Viruses cause stunting of the plant, so buy virus-resistant cultivars or certified stock. Anthracnose causes blackish blotches on leaves and fruits. Aphids spread diseases, so spray with insecticidal soap.

Pick raspberries as they ripen. Picking will help encourage more raspberries to form, but don't pick while they are wet. Put them into the refrigerator immediately after picking—they do not keep well.

BELOW LEFT A loganberry, which is a cross between a raspberry and a blackberry.

BELOW RIGHT 'Autumn Bliss,' a heavy-cropping, late-fruiting raspberry.

HARVESTING

3 cups gooseberries
½ cup sugar
6 elderflower heads
juice of 1 lemon and zest of half
1¼ cups sour cream
sprigs of mint to decorate

gooseberry and elderflower fool

Stew the gooseberries in a pan in a little water. Allow them to simmer until soft. Add the sugar and dissolve it over the heat while stirring. Wash the elderflower heads and wrap them in muslin, tied up like a giant tea bag. Drop the elderflower bag into the mixture and add the lemon juice and zest. Cook for an additional five minutes, squashing the elderflowers down with the back of the spoon. Remove the bag and sieve the gooseberries into a bowl. Fold in the cream gently. Pour into individual dishes, decorate with mint, and chill for an hour before serving.

1 cup raspberries
1 cup heavy cream
3 tbsp. of sugar
brown sugar to cover

raspberry crème brûlée

Although raspberries are particularly good as a base for this crème brûlée, you could use other tart fresh fruits in season. Black currants would be a good substitute, but unless they are very ripe, you will need to stew them lightly first with some sugar.

Divide the fruits into four ramekins. Beat the cream until it thickens, but is not solid. Stir in the sugar. Pour over the raspberries and leave to chill in the refrigerator for an hour or so. Just before serving, heat the broiler to the highest temperature, sprinkle the raw sugar on top of the ramekins to make a thin crust, and set under the broiler until the crust bubbles and browns. Allow to cool and serve.

4 cups black currants
½ cup sugar
2 cups heavy cream
1 egg white

black currant ice cream

If you have an ice cream maker, it will produce the best results. Other fruits can be used in place of the black currants—strawberries or blueberries, for example.

Stew the black currants lightly with the sugar for three to four minutes, then purée in a blender. Stir in the lightly whisked cream. Pour into a plastic container and partially freeze. Stir. Whisk the egg white until stiff and fold into the mixture. Freeze again until the mixture is fully frozen. Serve with macaroons or almond cookies.

fruit coulis

You can make a fresh fruit sauce out of strawberries, raspberries, or currants. Wash and hull the fruits. Blend with the sugar and lemon juice in a blender. Sieve if the fruits have seeds. Pour into a freezer bag or container and freeze. Serve chilled (allow a couple of hours for it to thaw) with ice cream or Greek yogurt, for example.

1½ cups of fresh fruits: black currants, raspberries, and/or strawberries

3 tbsp. sugar

juice of 1 lemon

red fruit compote

Hull or pit and wash the fruits. Add enough brown sugar to sweeten, along with the lemon zest and juice. Add just enough water to cover, and simmer gently until just tender. Serve warm with crème fraîche.

3 cups soft red fruits: raspberries, currants, strawberries, plums, and/or cherries

3 tbsp. brown sugar

zest and juice of 1 lemon

red fruit salad with kirsch

Make a light syrup with the sugar and ¼ cup water. Allow to cool. Wash the fruits, slice the strawberries and grapes in half, and place the currants at the top and bottom. Pour the kirsch and the syrup over the fruits. Decorate with a sprig of mint.

3 cups mixed red fruits: strawberries, raspberries, black currants, blueberries, and/or black grapes

3 tbsp. sugar

liqueur glass of kirsch

sprig of mint

grapes

vitis vinifera

A grapevine is worth growing, even in colder climates, if only for the attractive canopy of foliage. It should be possible to get a crop of dessert grapes, though wine grapes require a high concentration of sugar, which occurs only if there is a long, hot summer. Grapevines will not fruit until they are at least three years old, so if you buy a young plant, you will have to wait some time before you can pick your first bunch of grapes.

VARIETIES

The most commonly grown wine grapes are cultivars of *Vitis vinifera*. In Europe, these are all grown on U.S. rootstock after phylloxera, an aphid, caused widespread damage. *Vitis* 'Brandt' is a commonly grown ornamental and edible grapevine, which produces small, black grapes; it is very vigorous and makes a useful wall cover. 'Müller-Thurgau' is a popular wine-making grape that produces a riesling-type wine.

CONTAINER SIZE

A good-sized half barrel or a Versailles tub is probably the best option for a grapevine.

CULTIVATION

Plant a grapevine in fall or spring. Position it against a west- or south-facing wall for maximum sunshine. You will need to train it across a trellis system of stakes and wires. Pruning a grapevine correctly is essential for fruit production, and there are two principal systems: the cordon and the Guyot method. Although the latter produces maximum fruit yield, for

Grapes do very well in containers, with the advantage that you can move the pot into a sunny position as the fruits start to ripen.

amateur growers the cordon method is easier. For this, you will need to stake the leading shoot to a strong cane and then train the lateral shoots, alternately right and left, to horizontal wires held against the wall or fence. In the first two years, in spring and summer, cut the lateral shoots back to three leaves. In the fall of the second year, shorten the leading shoot by half of the new growth and cut the laterals back to within 1 in. of the leading shoot. Then in the third and subsequent years, when the flowers appear, cut the lateral shoots back to two leaves beyond the flowers, and cut back any shoots off the main laterals to just one leaf, the aim being to keep just one bunch of grapes to each fruiting spur. As the vine develops, you can increase this in future years to two to three bunches on each fruiting spur. Once the vine has reached the necessary height, snip off the leading shoot.

From spring to fall, feed regularly with a high-potash, organic fertilizer to encourage fruiting. Remove leaves that cover trusses to expose the fruit to more sunlight. Water regularly throughout, and when the grapes start to ripen, net them to protect them from birds.

The most common problems are scale insects, bird damage, and mildews and molds.

HARVESTING

Depending on the type grown, grapes are normally harvested in early to midfall. Generally, they are fully ripe once the stem has started to turn slightly brown. The bunch of grapes is cut off the vine with a 2-in. stem to act as a handle.

GRAPES FOR THE TABLE

Nothing is more delicious than a bunch of homegrown grapes. Serve them with a salty cheese on a bed of vine leaves for dessert.

frosted grapes and other fruits and flowers

As a decoration for other desserts, you can frost individual fruits and edible flowers by painting each one with beaten egg white, and then dipping it in the sugar, holding the fruits or flowers with tweezers. Dry them on a sheet of baking parchment. You can store them for a day or two between sheets of waxed paper in an airtight container.

grapes, cherries, strawberries, currants, rose petals, pansies

1 egg white, beaten

superfine sugar

grape and pear salad

Slice, core, and halve the pears. Spread the outer surface of the pears with cream cheese, and cover with rows of halved grapes, arranged lengthwise until each pear is fully covered. Arrange the pear halves on a bed of lettuce and serve with cold chicken or ham.

3 pears

½ cup cream cheese

small bunch of grapes

½ head lettuce

vine leaves filled with cheese

Wash and dry the vine leaves, then blanch in boiling water for two minutes. Dry them again and place one cheese in the center of each leaf. Make a pocket of each one, wrapping it with raffia. Place on a cookie sheet, pour the olive oil over the pockets, and cook in a 425°F oven for ten minutes or until the cheese has started to melt. Serve decorated with halved tomatoes.

6 vine leaves

6 small goat cheeses with creamy flavor

3 tbsp. olive oil

12 cherry tomatoes

TREE FRUITS

You can grow all kinds of tree fruits very successfully in containers, particularly the dwarf varieties that are now available and are bred specifically for growing in limited space. All apple trees are propagated by grafting small pieces of the cultivar in question onto a basic rootstock. Those for container growing have an M27 rootstock, which produces a tree roughly fifteen percent of the full size. Whereas a standard tree will reach about 30 ft. and will not bear fruit for at least six years, these smaller trees will only reach about 5 ft. and will bear fruit in half the time. You can also buy "minarette" trees, which are ideal for containers. They are trained to a single tall stem and fruit well, although not as copiously as other types of trees.

Remember that many fruit trees—particularly apples, pears, and some plums—need a suitable partner tree that blooms at roughly the same time for pollination purposes, although a few varieties of plums are self-fertile.

If your fruit trees fail to fruit, check the nutrient and mineral content of the growing medium. Fruits need high levels of potassium and also calcium and boron. Too much nitrogen will lead to a lot of leaf growth but is not conducive to fruiting. A soil-test kit will indicate any nutrient deficiencies. A foliar feed using seaweed extract and a spoonful or two of gypsum should improve matters. Mulching the surface of the container will help to retain moisture.

All fruit trees need adequate amounts of sunlight to fruit. Secure staking helps to prevent windrock. Remember when planting that the graft unions of the cultivar to the rootstock—the bulge on the stem—

should be about 2 in. above the level of the growing medium, otherwise suckers may form.

When pruning fruit trees, bear in mind that they generally benefit from an open structure that allows air to circulate around the branches, so the aim is to develop a central leading shoot with widely spaced lateral branches that will bear the fruits on their side shoots. Prune apples and pears in early spring and pit fruits after the buds form.

If desired, you can train a container-grown tree into a fan, espalier, or cordon shape. With an espalier, the branches are trained at right angles at either side of the main leader; in a fan, the branches are at a forty-five-degree angle to the main leader; and with cordons, the leader itself is at a forty-five-degree angle. These training systems are useful when growing fruit trees against a wall or fence, as they take up little room while allowing the maximum amount of sunshine to reach the fruits.

Should you be so lucky as to have trees that bear too much fruit, it is a good idea to thin the fruits out, otherwise the weight of them may damage the branches. (Bear in mind that the first few years of any new fruit tree are lean, and do not expect a lot of fruit until several years have passed.) Large fruits can be thinned to about 6 in. apart and small fruits to about 3 in. apart.

All fruit trees are subject to a wide range of pests and diseases, making them more difficult to grow than most vegetables, herbs, and flowers. You can help increase resistance to attack by ensuring that plants are as healthy as possible and kept stress-free through regular and appropriate feeding and watering. If you net trees, you will ensure that the birds do not get the crop before you do. Grease bands around the trunk will help to prevent some pests. For others there is no form of organic control except extreme watchfulness, removing pests by hand, and removing diseased shoots and branches when first sighted. Chemical controls for most diseases do exist, but you have to weigh the pros and cons in your own situation before using them.

Plums are heavy-cropping fruits (those shown at left are 'Black Star'). The best to grow in containers are those with a dwarfing rootstock.

a p p l e s
malus domestica

Apples are the most popular fruits, and there is a wide range of cultivars bearing distinctly different types of apples, from sour cookers to sweet, dessert apples. Some trees have been grafted to produce a family tree, with three different apples on one rootstock. Some apple cultivars bear their fruits on spurs—side shoots of laterals—while others bear them on the tips of the branches. You will need to know which type you are dealing with in order to prune it properly. Instructions are normally given on the label of the fruit tree when you purchase it.

CULTIVARS

'Grenadier': soft, sour cooking apple; 'Cox's Orange Pippin': crisp, sweet, dessert apple, which keeps well; 'Worcester Pearmain': soft, sweet, dessert apple. The above will all pollinate each other.

CONTAINER SIZE

At least 18 in. across and 18 in. deep.

CULTIVATION

Plant in fall or early spring and cut the main shoot and the laterals back to one-third, and any side shoots back to four buds. Mulch the surface of the container to help retain moisture and make sure the container does not dry out after the buds form. Foliar feeding with seaweed extract will help to promote fruiting.

HARVESTING

Pick fruits from midfall to early winter, according to the variety. If you store apples, put them on racks in a cool, dry place; they should not touch each other. Alternatively, slice them and freeze them.

Apples are harvested from
late summer to midfall,
depending on the variety.
'Sunset' (left) is an early-fall
dessert apple.

pears

pyrus communis

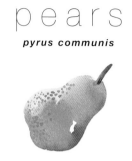

Pears lend themselves to all kinds of culinary treats. The trees are relatively easy to grow and more resistant to pests and diseases than many fruit trees, although frosts may damage flowers. Dwarf pears suitable for containers are grafted onto various rootstocks.

VARIETIES

As with other fruit trees, you will need to grow more than one cultivar of an appropriate type to ensure pollination takes place and fruits set—unless more than one cultivar is grafted on. 'Conference': long pear with good flavor; relatively trouble free; 'Comice': sweet dessert pear.

CONTAINER SIZE

At least 18in. in diameter and depth; repot to a container 24 in. or more in diameter in a couple of years.

CULTIVATION

Plant in late fall or early spring in a sunny, sheltered spot. Ensure that the growing medium has a pH of around 6.5. Pears need boron and manganese to fruit well, so if your tree fails to bear fruits, check the condition of the growing medium by doing a soil test. Make sure that the surface of the growing medium is well mulched with gravel, straw, or compost, as pears are susceptible to water loss. Dry conditions can cause the crop to abort completely. Prune pears as little as possible, because they are susceptible to diseases that enter through the pruning cuts. However, where possible, keep the structure of the tree open.

HARVESTING

Early pears will be ready from late summer, later varieties from midfall. If you pick pears while they are hard, they will ripen indoors.

Pear form and color can be varied, from the long, slender, green 'Conference' pears to this golden, rounded 'Onward' variety.

OTHER FRUITS

figs
ficus carica

A fig tree is worth growing for its singularly beautiful, hand-shaped foliage, regardless of whether it produces its green (try 'White Marseilles') or purple-brown (try 'Brown Turkey') fruits, which are both a valuable source of calcium. As the roots prefer to be restricted, a container is the ideal home for a fig tree, but you may need to repot it after a few years. Figs are generally low-maintenance plants. Net the fruits, however, if you do not want the birds to eat them.

cherries
prunus avium, p. cerasus

You can choose from sweet (*P. avium*) or sour cherries (*P. cerasus*). The latter are easier to grow, hardier, and self-fertile. Although some new varieties of sweet cherries are self-fertile, they generally need a compatible pollinator to set fruit—check the label to ensure you choose one that is compatible. Alternatively, you can buy a tree with two cultivars grafted onto it. Cherries are an excellent source of vitamins A and C, and riboflavin. The flesh of cherries can be purple, red, or yellow. Gisela 5 rootstock produces small trees suitable for containers. Of the varieties, choose 'Morello,' the best-known sour cherry, or 'Stella,' a self-fertile, sweet cherry. Plant up in a container at least 18 in. in diameter and depth, and repot to a container 24 in. in diameter in two years. Cherries will fruit in partial shade, but you will get the largest crop in full sun. Mulch well to prevent moisture loss and feed with organic fertilizer regularly from spring onward. Water cherries thoroughly and consistently once they start to fruit, otherwise the fruits may crack from overwatering or shrivel from underwatering. Prune cherries in the summer after fruiting to encourage the formation of next year's crop. Reduce the number of laterals on each main shoot to two, and cut back the side growth to three or four buds. Net the crop to protect it from the birds.

Plums, and their close cousins, damsons (*P. insititia*), are relatively hardy and largely self-fertile, but some will not stand hard winters and most will crop better if a suitable pollinator is grown nearby or grafted onto the same stock. Plums, which can be golden or purple-fleshed, are rich in vitamins A and C. You can also find hybrids of cherries and plums. Pixy is a dwarf rootstock onto which various cultivars are grafted, making it useful for container growing. Choose disease-resistant cultivars whenever possible. 'Crimson' is resistant to many diseases; 'Belle de Louvin' has purple fruits and is self fertile; and 'Opal' is a self-fertile early plum. Plant a young plum tree in a container at least 18in. in diameter and depth, and repot to a container 24 in. in diameter in two years. Site the container in a sheltered position in a sunny spot. The fruits are borne on spurs in the center of the tree, so prune to allow in as much sunlight as possible in either late fall or early spring. Mulch the surface of the container with an organic mulch to prevent moisture loss and make sure that the plums are kept well watered in the growing season. If the tree is cropping very heavily, thin the fruits. Net the tree to keep birds from taking the crop. Handle plums as little as possible, and leave the stalk on when picking.

plums
prunus domestica

Blueberries are hardy perennials that require acid conditions (with a pH level of 4 to 5.5). Container growing is therefore ideal if you live in an area with chalky soil, as you can control the acidity of the growing medium by using ericaceous compost mixed with an equal quantity of grit (to encourage free drainage). Blueberries must be fed with a fertilizer that contains no lime or calcium and should ideally be watered with rainwater in hard water areas. Mulch the surface of the container with bark chippings to retain moisture. Blueberries need little pruning, but in the second or third year, prune to remove roughly a quarter of the old wood. They can be either mid- or late-season fruiting. 'Bluecrop' is a good midseason variety.

blueberries
vaccinium sp.

3 cups apples and fresh, dried, or soaked apricots

juice and zest of 1 lemon

2 tbsp. butter

½ cup water

3 tbsp. sugar

2 cinnamon sticks

apple and apricot compote

This makes a rich compote, which goes very well with ice cream or yogurt. The addition of a small quantity of butter gives it more flavor and a creamier texture. You can make a very good plain apple sauce the same way, with a little lemon juice and grated zest, but using less water.

Slice the apples and apricots, and put them in the pan with the lemon juice and zest, and the butter. Cook over low heat in the butter for a few minutes, then add the water, sugar, and cinnamon. Simmer gently for fifteen minutes or until the fruits are just tender.

3 large tart apples

1 cup pancake batter (see page 39)

vegetable oil

3 tbsp. sugar

apple fritters

This recipe uses the shallow-frying method. You could also use the deep-frying method for the eggplant beignets, coating the apple slices with the beignet batter (see page 89). In either case, peel and core the apples and slice into rings, roughly ¾ in. thick. Dip the apples in the batter and fry in the oil until the batter is crisp and the apples soft. Dip in sugar and serve.

12 plums

5 heaping tbsp. mascarpone

4 tbsp. brown sugar

sprig of mint to decorate

broiled plums with mascarpone

This is adapted from Nigel Slater's recipe in *Real Food*. You could use ripe peaches instead, but the tartness of the plums goes particularly well with the sweetness of the mascarpone. If the plums are not fully ripe, put them on a cookie sheet and bake them whole in the oven at 350°F for about twenty minutes to soften them.

Cut the plums in half and remove the pits. Put them cut-side up on aluminum foil on a broiler pan. Cover with mascarpone. Sprinkle liberally with brown sugar. Broil for a few minutes until the sugar caramelizes. Allow to cool so that the sugar forms a hard crust and serve with a dollop of good-quality vanilla ice cream. Decorate each portion with a sprig of mint.

plum tart

You can make this fruit tart with whatever fruits you have available: cherries or gooseberries would be equally as good as plums. If the fruits are not particularly ripe or sweet, then stew them lightly with sugar first. Prick the pastry and cover with dried beans. Bake in a 350°F oven for twenty minutes. Allow to cool. Spread the fruits over the pastry base. Lightly beat together the eggs, sugar, lemon zest, and cream, and pour over the fruits. Cook in a moderate oven until firm to the touch, about twenty-five minutes.

1 piecrust

2 cups fruit: plums, gooseberries, or cherries

3 eggs

3 tbsp. sugar

zest of 1 lemon

½ cup heavy cream

pears in red wine

Peel the pears but leave the stalks on. Slice across the bottom of each to make a firm base and put the pears upside down in a small saucepan with the red wine and a similar quantity of water. Add the other ingredients and poach gently for twenty minutes or so, with the lid on, until the pears are just tender. Remove the cinnamon. Serve the pears in individual ramekins with the sauce spooned over them.

4 cups ripe pears

½ cup red wine

3 tbsp. brown sugar

zest of 1 lemon

grated nutmeg

stick of cinnamon

herbs and
edible flowers

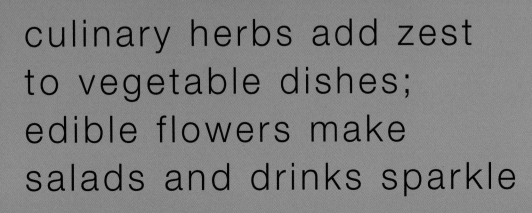

culinary herbs add zest
to vegetable dishes;
edible flowers make
salads and drinks sparkle

HERBS

Without a doubt, herbs are the best edible plants to grow in containers. They are well suited to the size, and provided you have a reasonably sunny place for them, you will be rewarded with some wonderful flavors and great benefits to your general health and well-being. The seeds of herbs such as dill and cilantro help the digestion of carbohydrates, while the green herbs—parsley, thyme, and marjoram—appear to help metabolize fats and oils, and are widely used with fried or fatty food. Although there is no reason why you should not experiment with some of the more unusual herbs, the most commonly used culinary herbs are a good place to start.

Everyone has particular favorites, but basil and parsley are the staple herbs used in most Western cooking, with cilantro the most popular addition to Eastern dishes. Cilantro is more difficult to grow in temperate climates than the other two. Although parsley is hardy, basil is tender and can be grown only as an annual in summer. The bush form of basil is somewhat hardier and will survive the winter in many downtown areas, which are usually warmer than more exposed areas.

Because most herbs will do just as well on a window ledge as anywhere else, if this is the only space you have available, grow them with a few of the smaller vegetables, such as lettuce, radishes, and arugula, and perhaps even some miniature vegetables, such as baby carrots or baby beets.

OPPOSITE   Marjoram (right) and parsley (far right) are easy-to-grow herbs.

chives
allium schoenoprasum

Chives are hardy, bulbous perennials and a member of the onion family. They grow to 8 in. tall, with long, slender leaves and small purple or mauve bell-shaped flowers borne in umbels in summer. 'Forescate' is slightly larger, growing to 18 in. tall.

purpose
The leaves are chopped for use in salads and egg dishes and as decoration for other dishes, such as broiled meat or fish. The characteristic "oniony" smell is caused by sulphur compounds, which are thought to benefit the circulatory and digestive systems.

cultivation
Grow chives in small containers or window boxes. Sow the seeds in spring, thinning to one plant per 6-in. pot in a sunny spot. Plants can be susceptible to downy mildew or attacks from onion flies, but they are generally fairly tough and pest and disease resistant.

dill
anethum graveolens

Dill is a hardy perennial and an attractive member of the umbellifer family, with branching flowerheads and feathery leaves. It does best in sun and will grow to about 4 ft. tall, but there is a cultivar called 'Fernleaf,' which is much smaller—about 18 in.

purpose
The prime value of dill in nutritional terms is to aid digestion and to dispel gas. The leaves, seeds, and oil are all used for culinary purposes.

cultivation
Sow the seeds in spring, thinning the plants to one per 6-in. pot or plant three to a 12-in. pot. Sow at intervals if you want a quantity of dill leaves or seeds. Gather the leaves in late spring or summer and the seeds in late summer.

cilantro
coriandrum sativum

A tender perennial, cilantro is grown in cold climates as an annual. It grows to about 12 in. high and will flourish in partial shade.

purpose
The leaves, seeds, and oil are all used in cooking, and it has pronounced antibacterial properties. The leaves and seeds are widely used in Asian cooking, as an aid to digestion as well as a flavoring.

cultivation
Sow the seeds in the spring and thin to three plants per 6-in. pot. Harvest the leaves in early summer and the seeds in late summer.

Cilantro has a tendency to bolt in hot weather, so move the pots to a more shady position if the temperature rises and keep the pots well watered.

This half-hardy tree will grow to 23 ft. or more in the wild, but it is slow growing and suited to containers. The evergreen leaves are dark green, oval, and glossy. In spring, established bay trees bear clusters of small yellow flowers.

bay
laurus nobilis

purpose

The leaves are highly aromatic and add flavor to soups and stews, either fresh or dried, usually in a bouquet garni of other herbs. Bay is reputed to have strong antiseptic properties and also aids digestion.

cultivation

Grow from cuttings taken in summer. Bay prefers sun but will grow in partial shade. Prune it in late summer. It can be trained into topiary shapes, such as simple balls or pyramids, or grown as a clear-stemmed standard tree.The clippings can be dried for winter use in the kitchen. Bay suffers from scale insect attacks, which manifest themselves with curled, blotched leaves. Remove any affected leaves at the very first signs and spray the bush with insecticidal soap as a deterrent.

BELOW (LEFT TO RIGHT) The small pinkish-mauve flowerhead of chives, the umbelliferous flowers of dill (*Anethum graveolens* 'Dukat'), and the aromatic evergreen leaves of bay.

mint

mentha spp.

There are many species and varieties of mint, a hardy perennial. The best known are spearmint (*Mentha spicata*) and peppermint (*M. x piperata*), which are widely used commercially. Plants grow to about 12 in. or more and the leaves are small and medium green. In cooking, mint adds a pleasant, slightly astringent flavor to vegetable dishes, such as potatoes and peas. Apple mint (*M. suaveolens*) has slightly hairier leaves than the more commonly grown spearmint and a good, fruity flavor.

purpose

The volatile oil, menthol, has long been used as an antiseptic and decongestant. Crushed mint leaves steeped in water make a good insect repellent when the liquid is used as a spray.

BELOW The slightly coarse-textured leaves of mint (below) and the smooth, soft, green leaves of basil (below right).

cultivation

Mint is invasive and tends to spread if grown in the garden, but containers are the ideal way to keep plants under control. Mint prefers damp, slightly shady conditions. Grow it from runners collected from other mint plants or propagate from seeds sown in spring.

This is the cook's delight. There are more than 150 varieties of basil, including varieties with deep purple leaves, such as 'Dark Opal.' A tender perennial, treated as an annual in cold climates, it grows to roughly 10 in. tall. Basil is among the most aromatic of herbs, and each variety has a slightly different flavor. Enthusiasts often grow several forms. The most common is the Italian basil, 'Genovese,' which is possibly the most aromatic; it makes excellent pesto.

purpose

Used as a flavoring for pasta and fish in particular.

cultivation

Sow seeds indoors in early spring and harden off outside when all danger of frost has passed. Site containers in full sun in a sheltered position and keep well watered. Snip off leaves as necessary. Remove any flowerheads.

This hardy perennial herb grows to about 12 in. tall and has highly aromatic, small, dark green leaves. There are numerous cultivars with slightly different heights and habits, including the yellow-leaved form, 'Aureum,' known as "golden oregano."

purpose

Excellent for flavoring soups, stews, and egg dishes.

cultivation

Sow seeds in mid to late spring and thin out to one plant to each 6-in. pot. It is fairly drought tolerant, but prefers partial shade because the leaves of some cultivars will scorch in full sun.

basil
ocimum basilicum

oregano
origanum majorana

parsley
petroselinum crispum

There are two principal types of parsley: curly-leaved, such as 'Moss Curled,' and flat-leaved, or Italian. Italian parsley has a slightly stronger flavor. Both grow to around 9 in. tall.

purpose

Parsley is a diuretic and helps to remove toxins from the body. Used in large quantities, it can be dangerous, but in the amounts normally used in cooking, it is perfectly safe. In culinary terms, it adds a fresh flavor to many buttery dishes.

cultivation

Sow the seeds in spring or summer. Parsley is notoriously slow to germinate—it can take six weeks—the process can be sped up by soaking the seeds overnight in hot water. Sow thinly in a 6-in. pot and thin out and transplant seedlings into other small pots once they are large enough to handle. Alternatively, grow it as an edging plant.

rosemary
rosmarinus officinalis

This is a valuable half-hardy shrub for container growing. Plants can be trained into neat standards or clipped into geometric shapes, growing naturally to about 5 ft. tall. The highly aromatic leaves are needlelike and gray-green in color, and pale blue flowers cover the uppermost shoots in early summer. There are many varieties, some lax and prostrate. The highly aromatic *R. officinalis* var. *angustissimus*, or Corsican rosemary, is tender but good for container growing.

purpose

Use rosemary to flavor lamb, chicken, fish, and potato dishes in particular. Put a sprig on a barbecue or broiler to scent the air and flavor the food. It purportedly improves circulation and aids memory.

cultivation

Rosemary grows very easily from summer cuttings and does best in alkaline conditions, so add a little lime to the standard compost mix. Grow it in full sun. It is splendidly drought tolerant. Clip it back in late summer to improve its frost resistance.

sage
salvia officinalis

This is another good half-hardy shrub for containers, particularly the purple-leaved variety 'Purpurascens.'

purpose

Use sage with fish, eggs, cheese, and beans, and in stuffings for fatty meat, such as pork or duck, or oily fish, as it helps the digestion of fats.

cultivation

Grow sage from cuttings taken in early summer. Position containers in full sun. Clip back in late summer to early fall.

thyme
***thymus* spp.**

Another of the truly aromatic herbs, thyme, a hardy perennial, has a long culinary history dating back to the Greeks and Romans; it grows naturally around the Mediterranean. The tiny leaves can be either green or variegated in gold or silver. The plants make a low, spreading mound about 6 in. tall. Bluish-purple flowers appear in midsummer.

purpose

Thyme helps in the digestion of fatty foods, such as pork or goose, and is excellent for stuffing poultry and other white meats. It is also good with cheese and eggs. Thyme is claimed to be a deterrent to flea beetles and cabbage pests.

cultivation

Grow from cuttings taken in summer. Position containers in full sun and use a layer of gravel as a mulch around the crowns of the plants. Harvest the shoots in summer, after flowering, cutting roughly two-thirds from each stem. This will not only give you thyme for drying over winter but will encourage more bushiness in the plants.

BELOW (LEFT TO RIGHT)
A variegated sage (*Salvia officinalis* 'Tricolor') and thyme are shown below.

EDIBLE FLOWERS

There are a number of flowers that can safely be eaten, and some even have medicinal properties. Grow a few edible flowers not only to decorate salads and other dishes, but also to introduce some color into the planting. Most of them do not have a great flavor, but a few flowers or petals on a summer salad makes it look more decorative. Zucchini flowers are delicious fried in light batter.

Some edible flowers are familiar, simply as the flowering element of an edible plant, such as chicory or zucchini. Others are slightly unexpected; who would have thought that the somewhat virulently colored daylily was safe to eat? Flowers can also be candied as decorations for cakes and puddings, and individual flowers can be frozen into ice cubes for use in summer drinks and punches, or frozen into an ice bowl as an attractive container for a chilled or frozen dessert. To do this, fill a pudding bowl two-thirds full with water, add the flowers, and then place another slightly smaller bowl inside it, weighted down to keep it from floating. Put the whole ensemble in the freezer for eight hours. When it is fully frozen, remove the inner bowl.

Don't overdo the use of flowers in salads; use just one or two as decoration. If possible, pick them just before you are ready to serve the dish. The flowers that follow are all suitable for growing in containers.

RIGHT Marigolds (*Calendula officinalis*) can be used to decorate salads; they are also a deterrent to whiteflies.

borage
borago officinalis

This tough, hardy annual with large, slightly hairy leaves has a rather untidy habit but startlingly beautiful cerulean-blue flowers. It grows to about 24 in. tall. You can add borage flowers to summer drinks and cocktails.

One unusual way to decorate drinks with borage is to freeze the individual flowers into ice cubes. Drop a flower into the water in each section of the tray before freezing it. (You can use other small, edible flowers, too.)

cultivation
Sow seeds in 6-in.-diameter pots and thin to two to three seedlings to each pot. Then allow the strongest to grow on. Alternatively, take root cuttings from an established plant in spring. Cut short sections of root, about 3 in. long, and insert into a pot of compost and sharp sand, with the crown end uppermost. Borage prefers sun but will cope with partial shade. Keep it well watered.

pot marigold
calendula officinalis

A fast-growing annual, pot marigold grows to about 18 in. tall, although there are dwarf varieties, such as 'Fiesta Gitana,' which are much smaller. They have daisy-like single or double flowerheads, composed of many tiny petals in bright orange, yellow, gold, or cream, depending on the variety: 'Indian Prince' has dark orange flowers; 'Lemon Queen' has double, lemon-colored ones. They have a long flowering season, from midsummer through fall.

cultivation
Sow the seeds in small pots in spring or fall—put cloches over the pots if you live in a cold climate. Pinch out the leading shoots once the plants are a few inches tall to encourage them to bush out and more flowers to form on lateral shoots.

zucchini
cucurbita pepo

The bright orange flowers of zucchini are edible, along with the attractive fruits (see pages 79–81 for cultivation information). Since the male flowers do not produce fruit, eating some of them while leaving enough for pollination purposes maximizes the usefulness of the plant.

nasturtium
tropaeolum majus

This vigorous annual climber has kidney-shaped, light green, large, slightly waxy leaves and exotic-looking, large, spurred flowers in red, orange or yellow, from summer to autumn. The flowers, the seeds, and the leaves are all edible, and the leaves are a rich source of vitamin C.

The plants need support on a frame, wire netting, or similar upright structure, although there are small bush nasturtiums that require no support, for example, the very attractive 'Empress of India,' which has slightly smaller than usual, purplish-green leaves and deep red flowers. It will normally make a clump about 10 in. high and wide.

cultivation

Sow the seeds in warmth in spring in small 6-in. pots and transplant into larger pots after frosts are over. Alternatively, use them to edge other climbing vegetables. If you are short of space, plant them in hanging baskets. Keep them well watered.

Pansies come in many forms, but the smaller, flowered ones are probably the most attractive for decorating salads. You can find pansies that flower in the winter, as well as in spring and summer. Most pansies grow to about 6 in. in height, spreading to around 10 in. They have a lax habit, making them a good choice for hanging baskets.

cultivation

Sow the seeds of winter pansies in summer and of spring-flowering ones in late winter. Pansies need frequent watering, particularly when in flower.

pansy
viola spp.

BELOW (FROM LEFT TO RIGHT)
A zucchini flower, nasturtium flowers, and a pansy.

FOR THE PANTRY

It just might happen that you have too many fruits or vegetables to eat immediately, in which case the most sensible thing you can do is to store them for later use, by freezing or by storing (for root vegetables, apples, and pears). Alternatively, turn vegetables into soup or pickles, and fruits into jellies.

FREEZING

Some surplus vegetables can be successfully frozen. These include whole green beans, fava beans, peas, peppers, and chilies. Tomatoes can be frozen if you puree them first. Vegetables that do not lend themselves to freezing can often be turned into soup, which freezes very successfully. Any fresh vegetables should be blanched before freezing. Plunge them into boiling water for a couple of minutes and then plunge them into cold water for the same length of time. Put the vegetables into a plastic freezer bag, suck out the air using a straw, and close and label the bag. To freeze soup, use airtight, self-closing, labeled bags.

STORING

Apples and pears can be kept for a while if they are laid out on a wooden rack in a cool, dry, dark place. Potatoes and other root vegetables keep best stored in a cool, dry place in a paper or burlap sack so that they do not sweat and rot. Hang underripe tomatoes and peppers in a cool, dry place to ripen on the vine.

Many fruits can be made into good-quality jellies. Some are not as high in pectin—which helps them to set—as others. Those that lack pectin can either be combined with those that have more of it, or you can add lemon zest and juice, which will improve setting. Those fruits containing the most pectin are apples, black currants, plums, and gooseberries; those with medium setting ability are blueberries, blackberries, and raspberries; and those with poor setting ability are strawberries and cherries.

The ratio of sugar to water and rapid boiling are the keys to setting ability. Some fruit will set much more quickly than others. If the jelly doesn't set as well as it should, keep it in the refrigerator, which will keep mold from forming—a common feature in jelly that has not set fully. When making jelly, remember to sterilize the jars properly and be sure to allow the jars to cool completely before sealing them because any condensation will quickly turn to mold. You will get roughly 5 lbs. of jelly for every 3 lbs. of sugar.

Making pickles and chutneys out of your own produce is very satisfying. The results also make good presents, with the added cachet that you grew the ingredients yourself! Salt is the element that does the preserving, so do not eat too many pickles if you need to avoid salt for medical reasons.

JELLIES

BELOW LEFT A glut of tomatoes can be used to make tomato sauce for pasta, which can then be frozen for later use.

BELOW RIGHT Raspberries can be frozen or used for jelly.

PRESERVES

USEFUL RECIPES

green tomato chutney

2 cups green tomatoes
1 sour apple
1 onion
½ cup raisins
1 in. root ginger, grated
1 tsp. salt
¼ cup vinegar
2 tbsp. brown sugar

Skin the tomatoes, peel, core and chop the apple, and peel and chop the onions. Mix together with the grated ginger and raisins. Bring the vinegar, sugar, and seasoning to a boil in a thick-bottomed saucepan. Add the ingredients and simmer gently until the mixture thickens. Pour into heated jars and sterilize in a moderate oven for thirty minutes. Allow to cool and then seal.

mixed fruit jelly

4 cups mixed fruits: gooseberries, raspberries, and/or currants
4 cups sugar
2 cups water

Remove the tops and bottoms of the gooseberries, and wash the other fruits, removing any stalks or hulls. Put all the fruit, sugar, and water in the saucepan and heat slowly to dissolve the sugar and soften the fruits. Sterilize the jars by washing them thoroughly and then putting them in a warm oven to dry out. Boil the jelly on a fast boil until it sets. Test the jelly every five minutes or so for setting by spooning a small amount onto a china saucer and allowing it to cool. If it wrinkles when you push it with the spoon, it is set sufficiently. Spoon the jelly into the jars, allow it to cool, and then seal and label the jars.

vinaigrette dressing

6 tbsp. extra-virgin olive oil
2 tbsp. wine vinegar
½ tsp. strong mustard
pinch of sugar
seasoning

A good, basic vinaigrette dressing makes all the difference to any salad. Simply shake the ingredients up in a screw-top container. Use as much as you need and keep the rest in the refrigerator—it will last for a week or so. You can vary the dressing by using lemon instead of vinegar, or by using specially flavored oils and vinegars. Walnut oil with raspberry wine vinegar is a winning combination. For a sweeter taste, use a little balsamic vinegar instead of normal wine vinegar.

basic soup recipe

Wash, peel, and cube the vegetables. Peel and chop the onion. Add the onion and garlic to a thick-bottomed saucepan and cook over low heat in the oil for a few minutes. Add the vegetables and cook for an additional few minutes, then add the seasoning, stock, and herbs. Simmer until the vegetables are just tender. Blend briefly and add cream or yogurt, as desired. Decorate with a few herbs. It is best not to serve soup piping hot or much of the flavor will be lost.

3 cups mixed vegetables: potatoes and artichokes or leeks

1 onion

1 clove garlic, crushed

1 tbsp. olive oil

seasoning

3½ cups stock

1 tbsp. fresh herbs, chopped

2 tbsp. light cream or yogurt

green herb sauce

If you do not want to make a white sauce, try this one instead. It is excellent with fish or baked or boiled ham. It is derived from a recipe by Claire Macdonald of Macdonald's Cream and Chive Sauce.

Put the cream in the saucepan with the lemon juice and heat gently for a few minutes. Stir in the chopped herbs, which will turn it a delicate green, add the seasoning, and serve warm with fish or chicken dishes.

1 cup heavy cream

squeeze of lemon juice

3 tbsp. chives, parsley, and arugula, chopped

seasoning to taste

organic growing media and fertilizers

The aim of organic gardening is to garden with nature, rather than against it, taking as little as possible from the natural environment and replacing what you do take. The following is a brief guide to some of the organic products you can buy or create.

growing media

Look for growing media that are either peat-free or do not use freshly dug peat (biproducts of water filtration plants contain peat, for example) to prevent the further depletion of natural peat bogs. There are various substitutes, based on substances such as coir or brewer's spent grains, that can be employed as a base, although they will need supplementary fertilizers, as they lack the fertilizing ingredients of natural peat. Organic gardening organizations usually provide their own recommended mixes. In addition to the usual range of ready-made organic seed and potting composts, you can buy organic grow bags.

If you want to make up your own growing medium, then make up a mix using seven parts of clean loam to three parts coir and two parts coarse grit. Add 1 oz. garden lime and 6 oz. blood, fish, and bone meal per bucketful of growing medium. A sowing mix can be made with two parts each loam and coir, and one part grit, with 2 oz. bone meal and 1 oz. garden lime per bucketful. The nutrient element in these growing media will last for four to six weeks; after that you will need to add your own nutrients.

drainage issues

If your growing medium is too heavy for certain purposes, for example, raising seedlings, you can add grit or perlite to improve its drainage ability. In other cases, such as for hanging baskets that dry out rapidly, you can improve the moisture-retaining qualities of the growing medium by adding special seaweed-meal moisture-retainer with the compost. It works in a similar way to nonorganic, moisture-retaining crystals.

fertilizers

There is a growing range of organic fertilizers, some general purpose and some formulated, to provide appropriate feeds for plants with particular needs, such as to promote fruiting. The rates of application are indicated by the manufacturer, and should be adhered to. Adding extra for luck can result in problems!

Among the many different organic fertilizers at your disposal are those based on seaweed. For container gardening, liquid seaweed extract is ideal, as it can be used either as a soil improver or foliar feed, and is quicker acting than seaweed meal, which is normally mixed in with the growing medium. It contains natural plant growth stimulants and an extensive range of trace elements that help plants to take up the nutrients. Other good natural fertilizers are liquid feeds based on comfrey or farmyard manure. General organic fertilizers for adding nitrogen and phosphates are often made up from a mixture of bone meal, dried blood, and farmyard manure.

glossary

annual Plant that completes its life cycle in one season.

biennial Plant that completes its life cyle in two years, growing in the first year and flowering and fruiting in the second.

cloche Glass or plastic structure which protects plants from cold weather and pests.

cordon Trained plant in which the growth is restricted to one leading stem—often used for fruit trees.

F1 hybrid Used to describe the first generation offspring of a cross between two genetically distinct parent plants.

half-hardy Used to describe a plant that can tolerate temperatures just below freezing for short periods only.

hardy Used to describe a plant that can tolerate temperatures below freezing for long periods.

hybrid Naturally occurring or artificially created offspring of two genetically different parent plants.

open pollination Pollination that occurs naturally in the wild.

peat Naturally occurring, moisture-retentive, rich, organic matter used for potting compost and derived from sedge peat or sphagnum peat. Peat substitutes, such as coir (coconut fiber), garden or mushroom compost, bark chippings, brewery grain residue, and leaf mulch are more environmentally friendly alternatives.

perennial Nonwoody plant that lives for two or more growing seasons.

perlite Granules of minerals added to compost to improve aeration and/or drainage.

pH Measure of acidity or alkalinity. Most garden plants prefer neutral to slightly acidic conditions with a pH of between 6 and 7.

pinch out To remove leading shoots to encourage bushiness or to prevent further growth (also known as "stopping").

potting compost Well-drained but moisture-retentive growing medium.

pruning Removal of surplus growth to improve shape of plant or to encourage flower/fruit production.

spur pruning A system of shortening the lateral shoots in order to stimulate flower or fruit bud production.

tender Used to describe a plant that cannot tolerate conditions below freezing.

suppliers

Ace
2200 Kensington Ct.
Oak Brook, IL 60523-2100
(630) 990-6600
www.acehardware.com

Gardener's Supply Company
128 Intervale Road
Burlington, VT 05401
(888) 833-1412
www.gardeners.com

Home Depot
2455 Pace Ferry Rd.
Atlanta, GA 30339
(800) 430-3376
www.homedepot.com

House 2 Home
3345 Michelson Drive
Irvine, CA 92612
(877) 980-7467
www.house2home.com

IKEA
www.ikea.com

Lowe's Home Improvement Warehouse
P.O. Box 1111
North Wilkesboro, NC 28656
(800) 44-LOWES
www.lowes.com

Plow & Hearth
(800) 494-7544
www.plowhearth.com

Restoration Hardware
15 Koch Road, Suite J
Corte Madera, CA 94925-1240
(800) 816-0969
www.restorationhardware.com

Seeds of Change
(888) 762-7333
www.seedsofchange.com

Smith & Hawken
(800) 940-1170
www.smithandhawken.com

Target
(888) 304-4000
www.target.com

True Value Hardware
8600 W. Bryn Mawr Avenue
Chicago, IL 60631-3505
(773) 695-5000
www.truevalue.com

index

ACKNOWLEDGMENTS

The author would like to thank the following: Steve Wooster for his superb
photographs, Madeleine David for her captivating illustrations, and Anne Wilson for her
elegant design; John Wingate, chairman of Golders Green Allotment Association, for
growing some of the vegetables and herbs in containers; the HDRA for the use of their
library and Maggi Brown in particular for her helpful comments on the text; Val Bradley
and Carole Handslip for their useful comments and contributions; Corinne Asghar and
Lydia Darbyshire for their editorial work; Marie Lorimer for the index; and Ken Muir for
information on fruit growing. Last but not least, thanks to the late Frances Lincoln and
her staff, in particular Anne Fraser, Jo Christian, Anne Askwith, Becky Clarke, and
Michael Brunström. Thanks, too, to Ginny Surtees, who commissioned this book.

PHOTOGRAPHY CREDITS

All photographs copyright © Steven Wooster except for the following, all
copyright © the Garden Picture Library: p. 30 David Cavagnaro/GPL; p. 31 Michael
Howes/GPL; p. 73 Phlippe Bonduel/GPL; p 94 Friedrich Strauss/GPL; p. 95 John
Glover/GPL; p 109 Friedrich Strauss/GPL.